Dynamic Duos
By John Guzzetta

© 2018 Spiritbuilding Publishing
All rights reserved. No part of this book may be reproduced in any form without the written permission of the publisher.

Published by
Spiritbuilding Publishing
15591 N State Rd 9
Summitville, IN 46070

Printed in the United States of America
DYNAMIC DUOS
By John Guzzetta

ISBN 978-0-9990684-2-7

Spiritual "equipment" for the contest of life

Table of Contents

1 | The Couple
The Basic Unit of Human Experience 1

2 | Adam & Eve
Made for Each Other 8

3 | Isaac & Rebekah, Samson & Delilah
The Second Most Important Decision You'll Ever Make 15

4 | Amram & Jochebed
Raising Faithful Kids in a World Out to Get Them 22

5 | Abigail & Nabal
How to Fight So You Both Win 31

6 | Abraham & Sarah
The Gift of Submission 39

7 | The Shulammite Girl & Her Shepherd Boy
Marriage and Sexuality 47

8 | David & Bathsheba
Protecting Your Marriage 55

9 | Herod & Herodias
The Tragedy of Divorce and Remarriage 62

10 | Hannah & Elkanah, Ruth & Boaz
My Spouse, My Greatest Encourager 70

11 | Job & His Wife, David & Michal, Ahab & Jezebel, Ananias & Sapphira
My Spouse, My Greatest Obstacle 76

12 | Hosea & Gomer
A Picture of God's Love for the Church 84

13 | Priscilla & Aquila
A Team for Christ 91

Dedication

For my dear wife Christine, who taught me the gospel and still does; and for our three wonderful children, Jonathan, Julianna, and Jessica.

Chapter One

The Couple:
The Basic Unit of Human Experience

The oldest institution in the world is not a company, not a bank, not a hotel, not a university, not a church denomination. It is not a nation, not a monarchy, not a dynasty. It is not a palace, not a pyramid, not an archeological ruin.

The oldest institution in the world is marriage!

As long as there have been human beings, there has been marriage. As long as this earth remains, until the resurrection, there will be marriage.

Marriage is one of three institutions that God Himself ordained for the benefit of mankind. God ordained government (Romans 13:1). God ordained the church (Matthew 16:18). And God ordained marriage. The family, though smaller in size than governments and the church, precedes the others. God created the family in the very beginning, in the Garden of Eden.

> The Lord God said, "It is not good for the man to be alone; I will make him a helper suitable for him." ... So the Lord God caused a deep sleep to fall upon the man, and he slept; then He took one of his ribs and closed up the flesh at that place. The Lord God fashioned into a woman the rib which He had taken from the man, and brought her to the man. The man said, "This is now bone of my bones, and flesh of my flesh; She shall be called Woman, because she was taken out of Man." For this reason a man shall leave his father and his mother, and be joined to his wife; and they shall become one flesh. And the man and his wife were both naked and were not ashamed (Genesis 2:18–25, NASB).

From that point forward, throughout all history, in every corner of the planet, in every culture and in every social or economic circumstance, the couple—a husband and a wife—has been the basic unit of human experience. Kings and queens marry. Peasants marry. Americans marry and Russians marry; sometimes they marry each other. People in the worst circumstances, in Dust Bowls and Great Depressions and even in concentration camps, find ways to perform wedding vows, endeavoring to create a pocket of happiness in the midst of a difficult world. God has given mankind a powerful blessing built on a firm commitment.

Marriage is God's holy will, designed not to stifle man, not to prevent him from having fun during his few short years upon the earth, but exactly the opposite—to provide him the most wonderful, exciting, and uplifting relationship two people can know (Ecclesiastes 9:9). Someone has wisely pointed out that marriage is the one feature of the Garden of Eden not taken away from man after the fall; in a sense, God has designed marriage to be a little piece of paradise on earth.

Why This Book?

In these thirteen lessons, I intend to present for your consideration several impressive couples of the Bible. It is my hope and prayer that this study will be beneficial to all. It is especially important that we learn God's will for our lives, as society drifts farther and faster from the biblical pattern.

If you are married, I hope that this study will give you a greater appreciation for the institution of marriage, a deeper understanding of what God intends to accomplish through your marriage. I hope that it will draw you closer to your spouse. This book will not discuss every single thing that could be said on creating a successful, joyful marriage. But by studying the biographies of couples God presents to us in Scripture, we will be prepared for much of what we will face.

If you are planning to be married, I hope that this study will give you the tools you need to become a good spouse, and to select a good spouse.

If you are not planning to marry at all, keep reading anyway. These couples are vital parts of the Bible story, and for that fact alone they are worth your time. Moreover, anyone can share these principles to other married couples or soon-to-be-married couples.

When I say "impressive" couples, I don't always mean positive. It would seem that for every good couple, like Priscilla and Aquila, there is a bad couple, like Ananias and Sapphira. For every Isaac and Rebekah, there is an Ahab and Jezebel. Yet, there is a saying that no one is worthless, for he can serve as a bad example. The inspired Scriptures present these couples—the good ones as well as the bad ones—to teach us something vital about the marriage relationship under the sovereignty of God. Their experiences "were written for our instruction, upon whom the ends of the ages have come" (1 Corinthians 10:11).

I must first discuss four things.

Homosexuality

First, a "couple" does not include two men or two women.

Great strides have been made by the homosexual agenda in the last decade or so, even in small Southern towns. Gay marriage is now the law of the land in all fifty states. Christians must keep watch on public policy discussions, questionable science, media programming, and educational efforts all the way down to the elementary school level. But for the sake of this brief section, there is only one necessary consideration: What does the Bible say about homosexuality?

God's will toward homosexuality is clear. In Genesis 1:27 God created man "male and female," and decreed in 2:21–25, "a man shall leave his father and his mother and be joined to his wife." God designed mankind to be sexually compatible; that males and females would be perfect counterparts in a family relationship (2:18) and naturally capable of reproduction. Human physiology on the physical and emotional level is a powerful witness to God's intention.

The Law of Moses declares, "You shall not lie with a male as one lies with a female; it is an abomination" (Leviticus 18:22). God showed His willingness to judge those involved in this sin when He destroyed the ancient valley of Sodom with fire and brimstone (Genesis 18). God identifies homosexuality as sinful in the New Testament as well (1 Timothy 1:9–10), and labels it an activity that must be repented of, lest it keep a person out of Heaven (1 Corinthians 6:9–10).

Scientists and psychologists can debate the nature of brain structure and lust. I am convinced that God does not put a person in a situation where he must sin (James 1:13–15; 1 Corinthians 10:13) whether by circumstance or by birth. Homosexuality is certainly a powerful temptation for some, but it does not become a sin unless it is acted on. Many simply refuse to accept or obey God's prohibitions, throwing them out along with the whole Bible. At least that is consistent. Worse, in my mind, are those who attempt to reconcile the Bible with homosexuality.

Do not be deceived. No matter what the government or society says about gay marriage, God's word trumps it. A couple is properly defined as a man and a woman.

Cohabitation

A "couple" in the context of this study does not include a man and woman living together without marriage. That arrangement has become very popular today. Statistics show that cohabitation is quickly gaining on the institution of marriage. In some ethnic groups, and in some countries, more children are born into non-married households than married households. A recent *Time* magazine cover story questioned whether or not marriage still made sense, or provided any benefit to society. The author observed, "In purely practical terms, marriage is just not as necessary as it used to be ... neither men nor women need to be married to have sex or companionship or professional success or respect or even children" (Belinda Luscombe, "Who Needs Marriage?" 11/29/2010). More and more, tying the knot of marriage seems to be pointless, especially as science conquers disease and unplanned pregnancy, and the tax code and social safety net disincentivize marriage.

Once again, I will ignore the conflicting social studies that, depending on who commissions them, find benefits or detriments with marriage. In the Bible, one can clearly see God's wisdom in making a firm commitment the foundation of couplehood rather than shallow emotional infatuation. The promise is a prerequisite to the living arrangement. Emotions are stronger and weaker all throughout a couple's life, depending on the various stresses they encounter. They "like" each other more or less at any given moment. But a godly married couple will always love each other. During trying times, the commitment to one another in the sight of God is what glues them together as a couple and a family until the circumstances change, the stresses are resolved, and they find themselves passionately head-over-heels once again.

Scripture demands marriage for those who would live together or enjoy a sexual relationship. Hebrews 13:4 says, "Marriage is to be held in honor among all, and the marriage bed is to be undefiled; for fornicators and adulterers God will judge." We have created euphemisms for it, but premarital sex is fornication, and it endangers one's fellowship with God.

A sexual relationship within the committed bonds of marriage is righteous, and it is more fulfilling. Finding a different woman every week is the selfish man's game; the real fun and challenge is providing for the same woman all her life!

Polygamy

When a friend of mine heard the title of this book, he sarcastically asked, "Which of Solomon's seven hundred wives or three hundred concubines will you include in your study of couples of the Bible?"

Point well taken! While God permitted polygamy in previous dispensations, Jesus points out that God's real intention always has been one woman, one man, for life (Matthew 19:4–5). Monogamy is the only marital arrangement God authorizes in the Christian dispensation.

Singlehood

Fourth, plugging oneself into a "couple" is not necessary to be blessed and to carry out a fulfilling life. Singlehood is a perfectly acceptable condition. While marriage is likely to be the experience for most people, there are some who can not get married, or should not get married, or simply don't want to get married.

The church must remember that just because a person decides not to marry doesn't mean there is anything wrong with him or her. In fact, Paul declares in 1 Corinthians 7:8, "I say to the unmarried and widows that it is good for them if they remain even as I." Paul was single (possibly a widower, based on his previous association with the Sanhedrin), and he encouraged others to remain single, too. There are many to whom God gave the gift of celibacy (such as Anna in Luke 2:36, 37), who have used that gift to serve God more fully than most married people, whose time is necessarily consumed with the responsibilities of family. Paul said,

> ... One who is unmarried is concerned about the things of the Lord, how he may please the Lord; but one who is married is concerned about the things of the world, how he may please his wife, and his interests are divided. The woman who is unmarried, and the virgin, is concerned about the things of the Lord, that she may be holy both in body and spirit; but one who is married is concerned about the things of the world, how she may please her husband. This I say for your own benefit; not to put a restraint upon you, but to promote what is appropriate and to secure undistracted devotion to the Lord (1 Corinthians 7:32–35).

In this matter of "to marry or not to marry," Paul is careful to say that he is merely expressing an opinion. "This I say by way of concession, not of command" (7:6); and, "concerning virgins I have no command of the Lord, but I give an opinion ..." (7:25).

Deciding to marry does not drop one down a spiritual notch. Paul repeatedly defended the institution of marriage (1 Corinthians 7:1–5, 9, 36). He mentioned that his cautions were "in view of the present distress" (7:26) which was likely a localized and temporary persecution. He labeled forced celibacy a "doctrine of demons" (1 Timothy 4:1–4) and in most cases recommended marriage. He advised marriage for widows under the age of sixty (1 Timothy 5:14), he required marriage for those who would lead the church as shepherds (1 Timothy 3:2), and he defended the right of ministers to marry and support their wives (1 Corinthians 9:5). Careful study shows that 1 Timothy 5:11–12 and Revelation 14:4 do not advocate celibacy.

But Paul also defended singlehood. He only spoke highly of it. He did not call it a curse; he called it a "gift" (1 Corinthians 7:7). Single people can be very powerful workers in God's house. Long ago, God said through the prophet Isaiah,

> Let not ... the eunuch say, "Behold, I am a dry tree."
> For thus says the Lord,
> "To the eunuchs who keep My Sabbaths,
> And choose what pleases Me,
> And hold fast My covenant,
> To them I will give in My house and within My walls a memorial,
> And a name better than that of sons and daughters;
> I will give them an everlasting name which will not be cut off"
>   (Isaiah 56:3–5).

There are occasions of loneliness and envy that attend the lives of single people. Of course, there are other stresses that they are spared. A single man once joked with me that he doesn't get to share someone's bedroom, but he doesn't have to share someone's bathroom, either! In any case, God assures the single person that he has important work to accomplish in the Lord's kingdom, work that will provide eternal blessing.

As we now turn to the couples held forth in the pages of the Bible, may all of us profit from this study.

The Basic Unit of Human Experience

Readings:
- Three passages that declare God's will regarding marriage and sexuality: Romans 1:22–28; 1 Corinthians 6:9–11; and Hebrews 13:4

Prep questions:
1. Why do all cultures recognize marriage?

2. Why does God present the stories of so many married couples in His word?

3. How do God's standard for couplehood and the world's standard differ?

4. What is one thing you hope to get from this study?

Chapter Two

Adam & Eve: Made for Each Other

In the beginning, Adam was incomplete. He named all the animals—by which I understand he examined each one and considered its qualities—but none "was suitable for him" (Genesis 2:20). Adam needed a partner, and no pet would do. He needed his equal in mind and spirit, and his compliment in body and attitude. Dogs are playful, but they can only offer their bellies for scratching, lick your face, and come when called. The very best can retrieve a stick. Animals provide affection, amusement, and maybe labor; but not love.

Only a fellow human being could satisfy Adam's needs. Thus, after God allowed Adam to deeply feel his loneliness, He fashioned from Adam's side the woman who would fill the yearning in his heart. By creating Eve, God provided a source of love and encouragement, as well as the means of procreation. God created the important sphere called the home. From this first couple came the pattern for all future couples.

Sadly, many still fall for the notion that marriage is the end of fulfillment rather than the beginning. Often, this notion comes from bad examples in the community, from one's own family, or from TV. A performer named Mike Birbiglia said, "I had always been against the idea of marriage. I didn't want to get married until I was sure that nothing else good could happen in my life!" (*This American Life,* radio program #379). He went on to explain that he never looked at his parents, or at any couple who had been married a long time, and thought that they seemed happy to be together.

This common but depressing view is not at all God's intention for marriage. Though husbands must learn to share a garage and wives must learn to share a bathroom, marriage is a great blessing. "He who finds a wife finds a good thing, and obtains favor from the Lord" (Proverbs 18:22). Husbands and wives trade in a tiny bit of their selfish desires in order to support one another, and to open up a huge and superior life of fulfillment that cannot be accessed any other way.

Some years ago, one of the young men in our congregation was facing his wedding date. We older guys kidnapped him. We forced him to walk around town in a T-shirt with hand-painted prison stripes, and a plastic ball and chain purchased from a costume store. We ribbed him repeatedly that he had come to the last enjoyable day of his life.

Honestly, though, not one of us believed it. Every one of us felt thankful to be married and rejoiced that he was about to enter the ranks of the married as well. Many years and two children later, he would certainly agree that his life took a turn for the better on that day, not a turn for the worse.

We learn several truths about God's intention for marriage by studying the very first couple, Adam and Eve.

A Spouse Truly Understands You
In the account of the creation of Adam and Eve, God said, "It is not good for the man to be alone; I will make him a helper suitable for him" (Genesis 2:18).

The old King James Version of this phrase was "a help meet for him," from an archaic use of the word "meet" as an adjective meaning "fitting" or "designed for." Eve was a compliment to Adam, a partner for Adam, a helper suitable for his needs. Woman was designed with man in mind, a fact which still today helps define the role of the sexes in the words of the New Testament authors (1 Timothy 2:13), but which also indicates their perfect correspondence.

It would be helpful for men to remember that wives are not inferior in any way, for "God created man in His own image, in the image of God He created him; male and female He created them" (Genesis 1:27). That is, both man and woman are human beings created in the image of God. Yes, the Bible designates certain differences in duties, and ordains leadership and submission in the marriage relationship. Jesus Christ does not regard women as less important (Galatians 3:28). Gender is a temporary fleshly condition which shall be abolished at the resurrection (Matthew 22:30). It is not God's intention, nor is it healthy for the home, for a man to fail to respect and value his wife as a "fellow heir" (1 Peter 3:7).

Helper doesn't mean slave or stepping stone. She helps him by standing together with Him, furthering his dreams, completing his family. He provides for her. When God brought Eve to Adam, he was very excited that God had finally created his true and perfect counterpart (2:23).

God knew what He was doing when He crafted Eve from Adam's side. It takes a spouse to know you and understand you.

It takes a spouse to listen to your ideas and express an opinion. It takes a spouse to appreciate your good qualities and steadfastly resist your bad qualities.

A Spouse Is Truly Devoted to You

Moses, the inspired chronicler of this Garden scene, draws a deduction for us: "for this cause a man shall leave his father and his mother, and shall cleave to his wife; and they shall become one flesh" (Genesis 2:24).

The word cleave is one of those rare words in the English language called a contronym, which has two definitions that are opposites. Cleave can mean to split apart, like the action of a hatchet; or it can mean to adhere to, like a tongue stuck to the roof of the mouth. I'm not sure how these opposite definitions came to be associated with one word, but perhaps it helps us appreciate the extreme quality of the commitment. There's no lukewarm complacency about this relationship. It's as if this sentence should come with sound effects: A man shall *cleave* to his wife!

They were so much a part of one another that "The man and his wife were both naked and were not ashamed" (2:25). Certainly that says something about the initial state of innocent bliss that Adam and Eve enjoyed. But even after the eyes of mankind were opened, a husband and wife share a state of complete togetherness that is closer than any other human relationship.

This commitment is at the heart of marriage. Though I enjoy a good on-screen romance as much as anyone, it is important to remember that much of the "love" we see displayed on screen is really infatuation. Feelings rise and fall like the waves. Love and commitment stand firm throughout these ups and downs. I heard a quotation years ago, though I can't figure out the source: "Infatuation is when you think your husband is as handsome as Tom Cruise, as amusing as Rodney Dangerfield, as intellectual as Albert Einstein, and as athletic as Hulk Hogan. Love is when you realize that your husband is as handsome as Albert Einstein, as intellectual as Hulk Hogan, as amusing as Tom Cruise, and as athletic as Rodney Dangerfield. But you love him anyway."

Becoming unsatisfied in marriage and convincing ourselves that we deserve something new and exciting is utterly selfish. Besides, what makes us think that our spouse keeps no list of things she could improve about us?

Commitment is the greatest part of the marriage. It is the guarantee that you both will weather the storms of life and support one another. It takes a spouse to walk through life hand in hand, to laugh and cry with, to grow old together. That's not something that fades with time or emotion. Remember the language of the vows: "in sickness and health … in want and plenty … for richer or poorer … for better or worse." They're not just said for tradition's sake—they are at the heart of a promise that joins a couple together as long as they both shall live.

A Spouse Makes You More Than You Were Before
There are some things in life that, when teamed up, become something greater than the individual parts. According to several anecdotal sources, horses hitched together pull about 20% more weight than the two horses can pull individually. Thus, if one horse can pull 1,000 lb., and another can pull 1,000 lb., hitched together they can pull not just 2,000 lb., but 2,400 lb. Some have suggested it has to do with having less of a pause between each hoof step. Two hands bench pressing a barbell can lift much more weight than the sum of each hand pressing dumbbells. I suspect part of it is psychological and part of it is from increased stability. Two people can lay a tile floor or cut up a downed tree or fold laundry much more than twice as fast as one person working alone. Cooperation keeps such jobs running smoothly. Companionship makes labor less of a drudgery.

A married couple is a powerful force, capable of much more than the sum of the individuals. There is a collection of interesting statistics on *www.phychpage.com*. Scientists have found, for example, that the mortality rate of single men is 250% higher than the mortality rate of married men. For single women, it's 50% higher. Though the statistics change from year to year, and have been subject to interpretation, most sociologists conclude that married people are happier, wealthier, safer, and healthier. Married people even heal from wounds faster. James A. Coan of the University of Virginia discovered that holding a spouse's hand during a painful procedure offsets the pain as much as painkilling drugs. I haven't tried it during the cutting part, but I know that when I came out of surgery, I was comforted by the appearance of my wife.

And most of these studies also found that these effects are not just as a result of living in close proximity to another person. The statistical benefits usually are *not* seen with those who merely cohabit; only with those who are married! There is something about the permanent nature of the commitment. I like the statement of Linda J. Waite and Maggie Gallagher in their book *The Case for Marriage: Why Married People Are Happier, Healthier, and Better-off Financially*, "Family experts have an obligation to let the public know: Sure, smoking kills, but so does divorce. Yes, a college education boosts a man's earnings, but so does getting and keeping a wife."

Solomon observed in Ecclesiastes 4:9–12:

> Two are better than one, because they have good return for their labor. For if either of them falls, the one will lift up his companion. But woe to the one who falls when there is not another to lift him up. Furthermore, if two lie down together they keep warm, but

how can one be warm alone? And if one can overpower him who is alone, two can resist him. A cord of three strands is not quickly torn apart.

While Solomon was mostly talking about business and society, his words are certainly applicable to the experience of marriage. When a man and woman work together as a team, there is very little they cannot accomplish, and there is very little that can come between them. They support each other's efforts and work toward each other's dreams. One may watch the kids while the other takes night classes. One may do the dishes while the other brings the kids home from piano lessons. One may take the car in for repairs while the other is laid up in bed sick. They pool their resources and share the cost of rent, food, and utilities. They prevent the ingress of temptations that would otherwise conquer those left alone and bored. Their mutual championing supplies a source of diligent labor for the Lord's church. Most importantly, they can provide the best possible environment for the nurturing and upbringing of children.

A Spouse Contributes to Your Rise or Fall
Salesmen often appear when the husband is not home; clerks strike when the wife is not wandering with him at the sporting goods store. This way, they can appeal to one's impulsiveness and weakness without the strength and good sense of his partner.

Satan, the crafty liar and murderer, appears to have focused his efforts on Eve alone. Satan turned Eve's eyes away from the zillions of trees from which she could eat, and turned her eyes toward the one tree from which she could not eat. He contradicted God's commands. He suggested that God was telling Eve half-truths and lies in order to withhold a world of excitement. He convinced her that there would be no penalty. Before long, she put aside her trust in God and drew close to the forbidden tree. Then, "She took from its fruit and ate; and she gave also to her husband" (3:6).

Disaster instantly entered the family. Their sense of innocence was lost. God confronted them both. He killed animals and clothed Adam and Eve with the skins. He cursed them with their own respective pains and difficulties. And, true to His word, on that very same day, they experienced spiritual death; they were separated from Him and cast out of the Garden. Satan had done great damage to the first family, and all the members of Adam's race have dealt with the consequences since.

One can attempt to assign blame. Paul, explaining his rationale for roles in the church, says that "it was not Adam who was deceived, but the woman being deceived fell into transgression" (1 Timothy 2:14). Of course, this means Adam in some ways has the greater sin, for he sinned presumptuously, willing to follow Eve rather than God. In any case, it proves to us that once we marry, our decisions affect more than just ourselves. Husbands and wives are like two trees whose roots have grown completely intertwined—it's almost impossible to poison or uproot one without also poisoning or uprooting the other. A drunken, pot-smoking husband may protest that he only hurts himself, but, in fact, he hurts his family. A materialistic wife may think she is owed a bigger diamond, but she prevents the family from becoming strong, stable, and debt-free. The connection between spouses is often so strong, that the other will follow into disaster without putting up much of a fight. Likewise, one strong spouse can keep the other focused on the right path.

God didn't want us to be alone. He saw fit to provide a perfect source of strength and support during the seventy or eighty years of our journey. Appreciate your spouse. Thank God for your spouse!

Made for Each Other

Readings:
- The story of Eve's creation in Genesis 2:18–25
- The Preacher's words on companionship in Ecclesiastes 4:9–12

Prep questions:
1. Have you found Proverbs 18:22 to be true in your experience, and in the experiences of your friends?

2. What is God's intention for marriage?

3. What can a married couple accomplish more effectively than a single person?

4. What can a spouse provide to improve the life of the other spouse, and the couple?

Chapter Three

Isaac & Rebekah
and
Samson & Delilah:
The Second Most Important Decision You'll Ever Make

Imagine that you are a top-notch sprinter with aspirations of participating in the next Olympic Games. But your wife is not a big supporter of your dreams. When you must wake up at 5:00 AM each morning to drive to the track and do an hour of sprinting before showering and going to work, she often moans and complains, and begs you to sleep in a little longer. When you must carefully monitor every calorie and nutrient in your diet, she keeps buying half-gallons of ice cream and eating them noisily on the couch in front of you, offering you bites. When you are faced with a budget crunch, she constantly and pointedly brings up how your trainers and sneakers and vitamin supplements add up to hundreds of dollars each month. You hesitate to bring up the fact that soon you will need to invest thousands more dollars to spend a week with a well-known coach, and attend a qualifying track meet on the other side of the country.

Clearly, your wife would be either the biggest supporter or the biggest obstacle to your Olympic goal.

Imagine that you are a piano prodigy, and your dream is to become a famous concert pianist. But your husband is not a big supporter of your dreams. When you must put in eight hours of practice each and every day, he often pleads with you to take a few hours off. He pokes fun that the scales aren't sounding any better than they did last week. He suggests—only half kidding—that you love that piano more than him. Sometimes, just to send a message, he blasts country music from the radio in the kitchen to disturb your etudes. When you leave every Wednesday at 2:00 p.m. to drive an hour to your instructor's studio, he is irritated that you refuse to allow your lesson to be interrupted for all but the direst emergencies. It becomes a hassle to plan every vacation, because you ask that wherever you stay features a lobby with access to a decent piano. He's so put out that he doesn't even bother to attend many of your recitals anymore. And the biggest fight of all happened when he realized how much you were spending on sheet music and lessons—enough to make payments on the truck he's always wanted. You hesitate to bring up the fact that you really need a new baby grand piano to take your skills up to the next level.

Clearly, your husband would be either the biggest supporter or obstacle to your goals.

In fact, it is obvious that any person with dreams of becoming a great athlete or musician is going to make that a key part of any dating relationship. He or she will tell any prospective spouse that the dream is such a priority that there must be no conflict, or a marriage is entirely out of the question. No one would think her crazy if she had said, "We had a good thing going, but he told me I had to choose him or the piano. I chose the piano!"

So then, why isn't this logic more carefully applied to a Christian seeking a spouse? If being a Christian and going to heaven are priorities for you, then why not let that be known unequivocally up front, that your relationship with God is such a priority that there must be no conflict, or else marriage is out of the question? A person with "like precious faith" will encourage you and participate with you on the road to heaven.

A person who does not see the value of faith will be like the passenger pulling the emergency brake while the driver is trying to accelerate. When you desire to attend worship services, he will complain that you are making the people at church more important than your family. He may even turn off the alarm to help you sleep in, or lay a guilt trip on you for departing the house alone. He will tell you that you are a ridiculous fanatic when you try to fit a worship service into a vacation. He will not respect the basis for your entertainment choices, and may even rub your nose in it as he spitefully turns up the volume on his own vile programming. There will be major disagreements on the moral behavior expected of children. And sacrificially contributing money to the needs of the saints when there are still toys to be purchased will be a constant sore point.

Mate Selection

It is not an exaggeration to say that choosing whom you will marry is the second most important decision in your life; only the choice to become a Christian is more important. Sadly, other decisions—such as what career to pursue, what city to live in, even what kind of car to drive—seem to get more attention than the character of the spouse to live with.

Preachers tend to present a lot of sermons on the evils of divorce, which is undoubtedly important. Divorce is sinful and should be avoided. God says in Malachi 2:16, "I hate divorce, says the Lord of hosts ... so take heed to your spirit, that you do not deal treacherously." But, if preachers would spend more time in the first place preaching on the importance of marriage, and how to have a good marriage, and how to select the kind of mate that will allow one to have a good marriage, then our church families would face the problem of divorce a lot less often. Mate selection needs to be discussed long before teenagers are old enough to fall in love.

In Genesis, God chose Abraham to receive the Messianic promise, in part for his potential as a guide to his family:

> For I have chosen him so that he may command his children and his household after him to keep the way of the Lord by doing righteousness and justice, so that the Lord may bring upon Abraham what He has spoken about him (Genesis 18:19).

When it came time for Abraham to help his son Isaac find a wife, he called his head steward and said,

> ... swear by the Lord, the God of heaven and the God of earth, that you shall not take a wife for my son from the daughters of the Canaanites, among whom I live, but you will go to my country and to my relatives, and take a wife for my son Isaac (Genesis 24:3–4).

The Canaanites were the people of the world among whom Abraham lived. Abraham had seen what happened to his poor nephew Lot's family before the destruction of Sodom and Gomorrah. This same society was full of immorality and idolatry. He did not want the Canaanites' worldly behavior tainting the dedication that his children would need in order to be faithful to God's promises. Abraham appreciated how powerful a wife's influence could be. With all this in mind, he put forth a great effort and expense to find a wife from a group of people who had a stronger belief in God.

Abraham realized what so many others failed to appreciate. Even Solomon, the wisest man who ever lived, was foolish in this regard.

> Now King Solomon loved many foreign women along with the daughter of Pharaoh: Moabite, Ammonite, Edomite, Sidonian, and Hittite women, from the nations concerning which the Lord had

said to the sons of Israel, "You shall not associate with them, nor shall they associate with you, for they will surely turn your heart away after their gods." ... For when Solomon was old, his wives turned his heart away after other gods; and his heart was not wholly devoted to the Lord his God. ... For Solomon went after Ashtoreth the goddess of the Sidonians, and after Milcom the detestable idol of the Ammonites. Solomon did what was evil in the sight of the Lord, and did not follow the Lord fully ... (1 Kings 11:1–8).

We modern American parents do not choose mates for our children in arranged marriages. But we must help our children learn the values that will allow them to make a good choice.

We must teach our children that marriage is a lifelong commitment (Matthew 19:4–6), and thus choosing well is important. There are no starter marriages for a Christian, no mulligans, no do-overs. One man, one woman, for life is the rule. This must be impressed upon our children at an early age, so that they take the decision very seriously.

We must teach our children that our spouse is the person who will be most influential on whether or not we go to heaven. We must teach our children that a devoted Christian makes the best possible spouse. A faithful Christian can be trusted with the checkbook and the credit cards. A faithful Christian will take seriously the admonition to raise children "in the discipline and instruction of the Lord" (Ephesians 6:4). A faithful Christian will tell the truth and will forgive a wrong.

And we must model these behaviors in our own marriages. It is a great blessing to deal with the person you live with for the rest of your life as a brother or sister in Christ. Wouldn't you want someone who knows how to selflessly love you because he or she knows the selfless love of Christ, doing "nothing from selfishness or empty conceit, but with humility of mind" regarding you as more important (Philippians 2:3–5)? Wouldn't you want to live under the same roof with someone for whom the will of Christ is nonnegotiable?

Lord, Show Me the One!
We must also look to God for help in selecting our mates. When Abraham's servant arrived, he immediately prayed to God to point out the woman that He saw fit for Isaac to marry.

> He said, "O Lord, the God of my master Abraham, please grant me success today, and show lovingkindness to my master Abraham. Be-

hold, I am standing by the spring, and the daughters of the men of
the city are coming out to draw water; now may it be that the girl to
whom I say, 'Please let down your jar so that I may drink,' and who
answers, 'Drink, and I will water your camels, also'—may she be
the one whom You have appointed for your servant Isaac" (Genesis
24:12–14).

God showed him Rebekah, a great and godly woman. If God loves to provide good things for His children, and if finding a wife is "a good thing" (Proverbs 18:22), and if it is such a huge component of our spiritual health, wouldn't God take special notice of such a prayer for a good spouse?

Now, I wouldn't suggest you repeat this maneuver exactly. Don't, for example, go to the mall say, "The next one who comes out of the automatic doors is the one you've picked for me, God." The next one out the doors could be a giraffe! Some people have a mistaken view of God's providence when it comes to the big decisions in life. Some people think that letting God lead means, basically, leaving the decision up to chance.

This is not the way God speaks to us today. God has revealed in His word the principles by which we can make informed and righteous decisions about every single dilemma or decision in our lives. Should I buy that car? Don't ask God to show you the right car by making the sunlight glint off it in just the right way, or by closing your eyes and pointing at random to a classified ad in the paper, or by saying "If I get approved for the loan, God is opening the door for me to buy it." None of these processes necessarily bear the stamp of approval of God's will; in fact, they may be Satan's tricks. Instead, ask God to help your make decisions by reading His word! When it comes to buying a car, you will need to consider priorities, whether or not you can afford it, and whether or not it will be beneficial to your family. God trusts His children to be good stewards, to use His guiding values to make the best choice.

Apply these decision-making principles to marriage, as well. People who marry based on infatuation or physical appearance alone often experience buyer's remorse—except that there is no return policy on marriage! Samson is a perfect negative example. We first meet him in Judges 14.

> Then Samson went down to Timnah and saw a woman in Timnah, one of the daughters of the Philistines. So he came back and told his father and mother, "I saw a woman in Timnah, one of the daughters of the Philistines; now therefore, get her for me as a wife." Then his father and his mother said to him, "Is there no woman among the

daughters of your relatives, or among all our people, that you go to take a wife from the uncircumcised Philistines?" But Samson said to his father, "Get her for me, for she looks good to me" (1–3).

The Philistines were idolaters, with whom God had commanded Israel to avoid marriage (Exodus 34:16; Deuteronomy 7:3). Even though God used this sinful decision as a means of exacting judgments upon the Philistines, it is recorded in Scripture to show us what disasters can result when physical appearances are the only standard we use when selecting a spouse.

Samson could not refuse a pretty face, for soon after he "loved a woman in the valley of Sorek, whose name was Delilah." Samson was a man of great physical strength, but of little self-control. For though it became quickly and abundantly clear that she was far more loyal to the Philistine nation than to Samson, he continued to stay with her, and eventually divulged to her the secret of his favor with God, and she wasted no time in handing him over to his tormenters. "The Lord had departed from him" (Judges 16:20) and his life was destroyed.

So, by all means, pray to God, "show me the one," and follow up by reading God's word. Look to God's standards to make your selection, not the standards of the world. In this case, an ounce of planning saves a lifetime of heartache. If the strongest man and the wisest man couldn't resist the negative pull of their spouses, what makes us think we can? Certainly do not ignore physical attraction; just don't stop there. Look for a spouse who will be a devoted Christian, a hard worker, a non-materialistic citizen of heaven, a loving companion. Look at standards of dress and behavior, speech and values, kindness and godliness. Consider the way they treat their parents, the wait staff, police officers, and strangers.

Find this and you will be happy in this life and pointed toward Paradise in the life to come!

The Second Most Important Decision You'll Ever Make

Readings:
- The story of how Isaac and Rebekah found one another in Genesis 24:1–28
- The story of how Samson chose mates in Judges 14:1–3 and 16:4–21
- The story of Solomon's wives' influence in 1 Kings 11:1–8

Prep questions:
1. What did Solomon's wives do to his relationship with God?

2. What were the top qualities Samson was looking for in a wife?

3. What were the top qualities Abraham was looking for in a wife for his son?

4. Practically speaking, how can you discover the spouse God has planned for you?

Chapter Four

Amram & Jochebed: Raising Kids in a World Out to Get Them

While the book of Exodus does not supply a lot of what we might call "parenting advice," the plight of one couple to raise their children in the realities of a dangerous world strikes me as parallel, in many ways, to our own modern situation.

Amram and Jochebed (their names are given in Numbers 26:59) were an Israelite couple living in Egyptian slavery. They already had two children, Aaron and Miriam. A new dynasty had come to power, and Pharaoh viewed the multitude of foreign Israelites as a threat. He made the Israelites "labor rigorously; and they made their lives bitter with hard labor in mortar and bricks and at all kinds of labor in the fields…" (Exodus 1:13–14). Pharaoh instructed the midwives to kill Israelite boys at birth. When they did not follow through, he issued a broad decree that "every son who is born you are to cast into the Nile" (1:22). Thus, all Israelite infant boys were in constant danger of being snatched from their mothers' arms and murdered.

It was into this environment that Amram and Jochebed welcomed their third child. Exodus 2:2–4 reports, "The woman conceived and bore a son; and when she saw that he was beautiful, she hid him for three months."

Now, any mother would find her child beautiful, and would naturally seek to protect him. But the Bible suggests there was more to her efforts than that Moses had rosy cheeks. In Stephen's commentary on this passage, found in Acts 7:20, he says Moses "was lovely in the sight of God, and he was nurtured three months in his father's home." Maybe in some way Jochebed sensed God's favor upon the child, or suspected his promising future as Israel's savior. The Hebrew writer praises Amram and Jochebed's decision as a work of faith, rather than instinct (Hebrews 11:23).

In any case, after three months, Jochebed could no longer hide the boy. So she took a step of faith.

> … She got him a wicker basked and covered it over with tar and pitch. Then she put the child into it and set it among the reeds by

the bank of the Nile. His sister [Miriam] stood at a distance to find out what would happen to him (Exodus 2:3-4).

She placed him in the calm pool at the edge of the Nile, in a spot where the noblewomen were known to bathe.

It is difficult to imagine the despair that would move a mother to give up her child, like a mother who leans out of a burning window to drop her infant into the arms of people gathered below. Jochebed risked the possibility that the Egyptian who found the child would simply toss him into the Nile; but that fate was all but certain if she kept him. The possibility of adoption into an Egyptian household was the only option. Jochebed sensed the danger—but she turned to God, and trusted that God would make a way.

Something amazing and providential happened. Pharaoh's own daughter found the baby and had pity, even though it was a Hebrew (Exodus 2:5-10). Miriam bravely spoke up, and offered to call a Hebrew woman to nurse the child; and of course, she called her own mother. Jochebed's actions saved her son's life, and, at the same time, allowed her to continue to raise him! Clearly we see God's hand in the outcome. Moses got all the privileges of growing up in Pharaoh's household (Acts 7:22), but he first learned the history of his people and of God's promises to Israel. When God's time came, Moses made the faithful choice (Hebrews 11:24-26) and became a powerful prophet and leader.

Modern Dangers
Thankfully, no one is threatening to literally drown the children born to Christian parents. But, in many ways, children are being raised in an increasingly hostile environment that threatens to drown them in wickedness. The spiritual dangers facing children are numerous and frightening!

The forces of darkness confront them at an ever earlier age. Parents lean over the crib and wonder how they will help their child navigate modern life. As the children get older, parents worry what they'll encounter at a friend's house, or what temptations they'll stumble across while innocently surfing the internet for a science project. Parents used to quiver at the thought of sending their kids to college—now, they quiver at the thought of sending them to middle school! Ellen Goodman wrote an editorial in which she pointed out that yesterday's parents were judged on whether they raised their children in accordance with the dominant cultural messages, while today's parents are judged on whether they raise their children in opposition to the dominant cultural messages. That's a huge, and important shift. We must battle our culture!

We are right to be concerned about these threats, and to take steps to protect our kids. There are real parallels between Pharaoh's efforts to destroy the children of Israel, and Satan's efforts to destroy the children of faith.

The story of Amram and Jochebed shows that we can look to God for help. I'm not suggesting we can abandon our kids to roam the streets and let God take the trouble of raising them. In fact, no one has a greater incentive to care for a child than his parents. Parents have a God-given responsibility to raise their children in the love and discipline of the Lord (Ephesians 6:4). No one else has that responsibility—not the school, not the government, not even the church. If a parent won't get serious about raising his own kids, he threatens their souls.

Still, we can quiet our worst fears, and rest assured that God is as concerned about their spiritual formation as we are, and He will help protect them. If God could bear Moses safely through the physical dangers of the Nile and the spiritual dangers of Egypt, God can bear our children through the dangers of 21st-century America. If God could watch over Moses in the Nile, God can watch over our kids at school. With committed, dedicated, and brave parents, and with God's help, even mistakes can become a vital part of their maturing into strong, faithful Christians.

Leaving behind Amram and Jochebed, here, in brief, are nine things God says will help us through this process.

Provide for Them

If we are going to bring children into this world, we must take seriously the responsibility to provide them with food, shelter, clothing, and education. Someone has calculated that it takes over $100K to bring a child from birth to high school graduation. I tend to dispute that number, but it isn't cheap. Children are an expense we must be prepared to meet through hard work and self-sacrifice. If we must drive jalopies so that our kids can soar (or simply have some lunch money) it's a worthy sacrifice. This is not the responsibility of grandparents or government.

We must work hard and exercise self-control to financially support our children. Deadbeat dads are an increasing problem. Others spend all their earnings on alcohol or hobbies, so that there is nothing left for the family. Dad must be a responsible breadwinner (Genesis 3:17-19; 2 Thessalonians 3:6-13; Ephesians 4:28). The Bible says, "if anyone does not provide for his own, and especially for those of his household, he has denied the faith, and is worse than an unbeliever" (1 Timothy 5:8).

Pass on the Faith to Them

Often I hear it said of wayward young adults, "His father was a great man in the church, I don't understand how his son turned out so differently!"

There are many factors involved, and free will is a big one (Ezekiel 18:4). But the above statement suggests that the faith is passed down genetically, like eye color and height. It is not. It is passed down through a diligent and conscientious effort to teach the faith to the younger generation. The Bible says, "Fathers, do not provoke your children to anger, but bring them up in the discipline and instruction of the Lord (Ephesians 6:4). Moses himself said, "You shall teach [God's word] diligently to your sons and shall talk of them when you sit in your house and when you walk by the way and when you lie down and when you rise up" (Deuteronomy 6:7).

Being a faithful Christian and being a good parent are two separate skills. Just because a parent attends all services, prays daily, and gives alms to the poor, does not automatically make him a proactive father.

Parenting requires the exertion of influence. That requires time, connection, and conversation. Instead of coming home and plopping down on the sofa to watch TV, or sitting at the dinner table with the newspaper, parents must get involved in children's lives in order to influence them. Ask them what happened during their day and don't take "Nothing" for an answer. Pledge that you will not fiddle with your own hobbies until you've spent time with the kids. Teach them around the dinner table and while driving down the road, and early in the morning and late at night before bed, when the opportunity presents itself with teachable moments. Schedule it when it does not.

Of all God's creatures, only human beings have the privilege of raising children and imparting to them character and wisdom for their lives. Mommy spiders do not teach their spiderlings how to spin intricate webs—they know how by innate programming (Job 39:13-17). The angels do not reproduce (Matthew 22:30). Even if we are not responsible for our children's choices, we are responsible for how we guide them and respond to them. We cannot force them to become God-fearing people. That's a decision they must make on their own. But we must help them to develop a faith of their own.

The Russian writer Leo Tolstoy recounts a scene in his short story, *Memoirs of a Lunatic,* which just may have been based on real life. The main character asks his aunt, "Why did they crucify Jesus?" She answered, "They were wicked." He asked, "But, wasn't He God?" Rather than taking this opportunity to explain the gospel, she said, "Be still. It's nine-o'clock, don't you hear the clock striking?" He persisted to ask, and she said, "Be quiet, I say, for I am going to the dining room to have tea now!" Episodes like this completely puzzle children; why parents would refuse to discuss something so important. We had better not allow our programs or hobbies keep us from instructing our children about the ways of God.

Three times in the history of Israel, God told the children of Israel that their kids were going to ask questions about spiritual things (Exodus 13:14; Deuteronomy 6:20; Joshua 4:6). God's advice was never to tell them to shut up, to tell them to ask their friends, to tell them to see if the preacher will preach about it, to tell them to go turn on the TV, but rather to explain it. A parent's responsibility is to fill his children's hearts with stories of God and His power, of God's care, of God's nature.

Prove to Be a Good Example

Teaching must be accompanied by a good example. While kids often do not do what we say, they almost always do what we do. Austin L. Sorensen once said, "A child is not likely to find a father in God unless he finds something of God in his father." Paul said that Timothy's faith came from the modeling of his mother and grandmother (2 Timothy 1:5).

Therefore, don't just talk about worshipping God; show what it means to worship God by doing it. Don't be one of those "do as I say not as I do" parents. Model Christianity in action.

Punish Them

Despite the modern notion that spanking is wrong, our Heavenly Father, the perfect parent, tells us that such punishment, and others like it, are helpful and necessary (Proverbs 22:15; 29:15). In fact, if we don't, then the outcome is much worse (Proverbs 19:18; 23:13–14; 13:24). Like the parent who spares a child the prick of a tetanus shot, and allows him to develop fatal lockjaw, we love our kids less if we refuse to discipline them (Hebrews 12:7–11; 1 Kings 1:5–6; 1 Samuel 2:12–14, 22).

Praise Them

It is easy to overdo discipline. Failing to express our love for our children gives them a perverted view of God, a God who is all frowns, no fellowship. We should praise them often!

Some parents do not pay attention to their children unless they require correction. Eventually, this becomes a frustrating cycle, for it is accurate to say that children prefer negative attention to no attention at all, and will misbehave if that's what it takes to spend time with mom or dad.

Play with Them

Good times between you and your child should outnumber the bad. Play with them. Be sure to devote time to taking your children on outings, running with them, and doing fun projects together. Find some activity that you can enjoy. And do not fall for the "quality time" myth that you don't have to spend very much time with your kids as long as it is packed with positive feelings—kids desire quantity time as well.

James Boswell, a famous author who lived from 1740–1795, often wrote about a special day in his childhood when his father took him fishing. The day was fixed in his mind, and he reflected upon many things his father had taught him in the course of their fishing experience together. It occurred to some later historian, after having read of that particular excursion so often, to go back and check the journal that Boswell's father kept, and determine what had been said about the fishing trip from the parental perspective. Turning to that date, the historian found only one sentence entered: "Gone fishing today with my son; a day wasted" (from *The Effective Father* by Gordon MacDonald).

Time spent with your children should never be considered time wasted. Sure, it may prevent you from getting the lawn mowed today or the garage cleaned, it may require you to come home early from the office and earn a little less this month, it may force you to miss your favorite TV show or put off your favorite hobby, but judging from what we see in the average American family, it is just about the best thing you can do with your time. We must change the way we look at children—not as a nuisance, but as a gift from God Himself (Psalm 127:3; Matthew 19:14).

Protect Them from the Worst Influences

I wanted my kids to know how to handle certain dangers. We taught them to swim so that they would be able to rescue themselves if they fell out of a boat or off a dock. We taught them how to operate a gun so that they would not be a victim of a stupid accident or curiosity. We did not tell them never to cross the street, but rather showed them how to safely check for traffic and ride their bikes.

But there are other dangers that we do not prepare our kids for—we just keep those dangers as far away from them as possible. No one that I know of allows their children to experiment with dynamite, figuring that some children have to learn the hard way! No, there are certain dangers that have no learning curve, that cause sudden and irreparable spiritual damage. These things must be kept away. Things like internet pornography, drugs, teen pregnancy, and the wrong crowd. Sometimes it requires drastic action, such as taking away the keys, shutting down the cable subscription, or even changing neighborhoods or schools.

Prepare Them for the Rest of What They'll Face

It's impossible to shield children from everything. Complete isolation is unrealistic anyway. Instead, good parents prepare children to face a world full of temptation and distraction.

Once upon a time, most of society agreed that certain temptations should be kept out of the way, in hidden places, where even slightly diligent parents could prevent their children from coming into contact with them. My folks didn't have to worry about what was on TV, about what I'd bump into at other kids' houses, about drugs or strangers, or that middle school girls would be enticing me into their rooms. Those days are over. Now, the adolescent landscape is mined with dangerous traps, secret ones in friends' homes and official ones in classrooms, and we must prepare our children to face them faithfully.

Pray for Them

Since human parents are finite beings, who cannot be everywhere at once, it is vital to request the help of our eternal all-seeing Father. Job, for example, habitually would offer up burnt offerings for his seven sons and three daughters (Job 1:2–5). Manoah and his wife prayed regarding Samson, "O Lord, please let the man of God whom You have sent come to us again, that he may teach us what to do for the boy who is to be born" (Judges 13:8). Ask for God's help!

If we would spend one-tenth of the time working toward our children's spiritual success as we do their academic and financial success, we would surely do well. I would rather have a faithful child than a wealthy child any day. Let's do our part to teach and protect our children. But then let's entrust them to a faithful Creator. Who knows? Maybe one day one of them will become, like Moses, just what his country needs.

And let us get started early! The other day I saw a topiary, two fichus trees with their trunks entwined into a braid. I soon realized that the artist didn't take two mature trees and twist them together. The artist would have taken two tender saplings and braided the trunks. While they are still young saplings, they are flexible. As they aged, they hardened and set into that pattern.

Many sociologists suggest that our children have largely become who they are going to be by age 14. Some put it earlier, some later. Two Harvard professors, James Q. Wilson and Richard Herrnstein, wrote a book called *Crime and Human Nature* and argued that the main indicators of a person who will lead a life of crime are all found before age six. I don't know how much to trust their numbers, and I don't know if they understand the power of the gospel, but I certainly see their point.

Kids grow up very quickly. There is no greater responsibility that God has given a couple than their children. Give it your utmost attention while you have the opportunity.

Raising Kids in a World Out to Get Them

Readings:
- The story of Amram and Jochebed in Exodus 2:1–12
- A bit on the duties of parenting, in Deuteronomy 6:6–7, Ephesians 6:1–4

Prep questions:

1. What are the most frightening things about our society and its influence on our children?

2. What can we do about those dangers?

3. Of the nine "P's of Parenting" touched on in this chapter, which one are you the best at?

4. Which area do you need to work on the most?

Chapter Five

Abagail & Nabal:
How to Fight So You Both Win

David had been anointed the next king of Israel, but Saul was still on the throne.

Saul attempted to hunt down and kill David, and David was forced to live in the wilderness. All Israel knew that David was a godly man, that he was the champion of the downtrodden, and that God would soon make him king. In 1 Samuel 25, David found a suitable hiding spot for his army in an area near the shepherds of a wealthy man named Nabal.

Months later, David heard that Nabal was shearing his enormous flock of sheep. According to the custom of the day, this was a festive occasion, when the owner would provide a lavish banquet for all the servants and shearers, to celebrate the bounty that was being brought in. It was a time of plenty and generosity.

David sent messengers to Nabal, asking for some food and drink to sustain his men in the wilderness. David pointed out that for many months his men had protected Nabal's shepherds. Often, when fighting men live in an area, they terrorize the locals. Not in this case. David's men had behaved themselves in a righteous manner. In fact, their presence helped Nabal's harvest be especially bountiful, since the flocks were well-protected from the depredations of enemies. This wasn't a shakedown; it was a request for help, an appeal to the sort of courtesy that one Israelite could expect from another. Furthermore, David's men were God's chosen ones, fighting the battles of God, and should have been able to expect assistance.

Nabal did not just refuse David's request. He insulted David and his men, sending his servants back both empty-handed and humiliated.

David, in a fit of anger, instructed his men to gird on their swords in order to exact vengeance against Nabal. David swore an oath that he would kill Nabal and all the males of his house (25:22)!

From this point on in the chapter, the author puts all of the focus on Nabal's wife Abigail. The author had already introduced the couple in verse 3:

> Now the man's name was Nabal, and his wife's name was
> Abigail. And the woman was intelligent and beautiful in

appearance, but the man was harsh and evil in his dealings, and he was a Calebite.

Nabal's insults prove that he did not accept the promises of God (25:10). He was unreasonable and unapproachable (v. 17), and also a drunk (v. 36). Abigail found out about Nabal's response from the servants, who came rushing to her side, saying, "... consider what you should do, for evil is plotted against our master and against all his household, and he is such a worthless man that no one can speak to him" (v. 17).

Abigail, who was a believer in God's promises to David, sprang into action in order to save her family. She gathered a rich offering of food and drink, loaded it on donkeys, and rode down the mountain to intercept David. When she spotted him, she dismounted and bowed before him with all the grace and humility that Nabal should have demonstrated. She did not grovel or make excuses. Instead, with great wisdom, she reminded David of his own preferred relationship with God (v. 29). She reminded him how God always fought David's battles for him. She pointed out that "shedding blood and avenging yourself by your own hand" (v. 26) would be completely out of David's character, and would in fact be unrighteous and sinful. Whether she deserved it or not, she assumed the blame for failing to see David's messengers and providing food, and asked David to accept her offering.

> Then David said to Abigail, "Blessed be the Lord God of Israel, who sent you this day to meet me, and blessed be your discernment, and blessed be you, who have kept me this day from bloodshed and from avenging myself by my own hand" (25:32–33).

David listened to Abigail's wise counsel, and praised her quick action and discernment. He accepted her correction, and indeed thanked God for sending her to talk him out of a bloodthirsty sin. David received the generous gift, and departed the mountain for his camp in peace.

Abigail still had to face her husband. She waited until morning when he had sobered up. When Nabal came to the realization of what had almost happened, "...his heart died within him so that he became as a stone. And about ten days later, it happened that the Lord struck Nabal and he died" (25:37–38).

When David heard about it, he once again thanked God for staying his hand through the wisdom of Abigail, and sent a marriage proposal to Abigail. She accepted, and became his third wife. While she spent time trudging about in the wilderness, she was destined to live in David's palace.

Unequally Yoked
Now, not all these stories have such a storybook ending, where God steps in and saves the woman from an ogre of a husband, and provides her the wonderful Prince Charming she deserves. Sometimes, a wife (or husband) finds herself "unequally yoked"—whether to a non-Christian, or to an under-committed Christian—and she must struggle all her adult life to serve God, to participate with her brethren, and bring up her children in the faith.

How can an Abigail share a roof with a Nabal? The first thing is to endure. Her husband, lacking knowledge of Jesus' word, and lacking an appreciation of the selfless love of Jesus' life, may be a challenge to live with, much less to love and respect. He may resist her efforts to go to services and offer a contribution, he may undermine her efforts to protect her children from media filth, he may laugh at her faith and question her motives, and he may fail to realize what a precious gift he possesses in a wife who loves God more than she loves him. Chained to such a man, she must put a lot of faith in Jesus' promise, "He who overcomes, I will grant to him to sit down with Me on My throne" (Revelation 3:21). In the aftermath of a stormy fight, or in the exasperation of another bitter disappointment, or when comparing her situation to situations of other families at church, she must remember 1 Peter 4:19, "Therefore, let those also who suffer according to the will of God shall entrust their souls to a faithful Creator in doing what is right." One day, you too will be swept up to the palace—the heavenly palace!

The second thing is to put God first. Compromise and flexibility will be necessary, but there are some lines that cannot be crossed. Sometimes in Christ, "a man's enemies will be the members of his household. He who loves father or mother more than Me is not worthy of Me" (Matthew 10:36–37).

Third is to hope and pray and gently work for a change of heart. If a spouse finds herself (or himself) in this situation, she can still be proactive. She must be committed to the marriage, but she can also be committed fully to God. Peter gives instruction:

> In the same way, you wives, be submissive to your own husbands so that even if any of them are disobedient to the word, they may be won without a word by the behavior of their wives, as they observe your chaste and respectful behavior (1 Peter 3:1–2).

It is a delicate dance to lead a person to whom you must also submit. A godly wife can sometimes guide her unbelieving husband toward the Lord, usually through example rather than nagging, and usually by appealing to the authority of God rather than her own wishes as a spouse. A wife may not be able to convince her husband to give up his drunken ways by harping on the damage it is doing to her and the family, but she can remind him what the Bible says about it; now he defies God, not her! As Paul says, in words that echo Abigail's situation, "... how do you know, O wife, whether you will save your husband? Or how to you know, O husband, whether you will save your wife?" (1 Corinthians 7:15–16). Abigail interceded on behalf of her family. She was able to save her children and her household, and in fact was able to save her husband for a time. Try to make an agreement to take the children to as many Bible classes and services as possible. Timothy's mother and grandmother managed to make of him a devoted gospel preacher despite his father's apparent unconcern (Acts 16:1; 2 Timothy 1:5). Try to make an arrangement to contribute some of your own income to the Lord. Try to explain, in gentle terms, why you do not want to participate in certain unrighteous things, and would like to participate in other wholesome things. Show how being a faithful Christian makes you a better spouse. There likely will have to be concessions, but do your best.

How to Fight So You Both Win
We have considered how an Abigail might make the most of her life with a Nabal. But even in great marriages, conflict occurs. Communication, if it is handled correctly, is the lifeline to explaining the problem and coming to terms. Let spouses argue in such a respectful way that they provide mutual support!

The interactions between Nabal and Abigail provide a negative example of disagreements in a marriage. Nabal had shut down all communication, robbing himself of her great and godly wisdom. Surely if Nabal had treated Abigail as respectfully as David did, they could have had a wonderful marriage. But instead, they had gotten to a point where they weren't talking at all. Many marriage counselors suggest that this is the last stage before complete marital breakdown. Most people think that marriages end with a big screaming match. But usually they end in apathy; when the two construct emotional walls and withdraw from one another.

In a historical context where most marriages were arranged, it's impossible to speculate on the first few days of Nabal and Abigail's union. Was it like so many of our marriages that begin with a whirlwind of excitement, and then slowly fade? Habits and traits that always had been there but were overshadowed by beauty and infatuation and adventure now emerge. And they are annoying! These behaviors begin to tear the couple apart, if they allow it.

No marriage is without conflict. An old country preacher once told me, "A man who says he never fights with his wife is probably lying about other things, too!" Any time two people live under the same roof—brothers and sisters growing up together, police officers assigned to the same squad car, hikers sharing a tent—there will be disagreements and friction.

You can unzip the tent and move your sleeping bag into the meadow, you can ask the sergeant for a new assignment, and you can look forward to the day when your sibling moves out and you get your own room, but there is no godly way to abandon a marriage. And so there must be a way for a husband and wife to express dissatisfaction and come to terms with problems. In my experience with couples and families, most disagreements come from one of the following six areas: handling money, raising children, spending time together, sex, in-laws, and household chores. Couples whose marriages stand the test of time learn how to voice a complaint in a trusting environment, hash it out, and come away with grace, forgiveness, understanding, and satisfaction. Happy couples and unhappy couples fight about exactly the same things; but they fight in very different ways. Happy couples fight in such a way that both win! Here are a few brief pointers, to save ourselves from experiencing the horrendous relationship of Abigail and Nabal.

Fight at the Right Time
Nabal was so unreasonable that everyone in the household was afraid to approach him. He needed to follow the words of James 1:19–20, "… be quick to hear, slow to speak, and slow to anger; for the anger of man does not achieve the righteousness of God." If a husband or wife starts a fight when one or both are acting like a raving lunatic, it is liable to make matters worse.

Instead, find a way to cool the tempers. Walk away for a time, think, get some fresh air, pray. I have a rule that I put in place after learning my lesson the hard way many times—I never send a negative e-mail the same day I write it. I wait until the next day, look at it afresh with a cooler head, and rephrase certain things that were too harsh or unfair. Sometimes I may delete whole paragraphs or decide not to send it at all. It's wise for married couples to pick their battles, and decide to leave a large part of their complaints unsaid—choosing rather to simply overlook the faults in their spouse, mindful that they have plenty of faults of their own.

Proverbs 29:8 says, "Scorners set a city aflame, but wise men turn away anger." If a whole city can be brought to ruins by the angry words of hot-tempered men, then certainly so can a family!

Never fight in public. Never fight in front of company. Do not fight when there is not going to be sufficient time to complete the discussion to both person's satisfaction. On the way to church, or when late getting out the door for a party, or two minutes before the babysitter arrives, are bad times to argue. Do not fight right before you head out the door for work. Do not fight when hungry, tired, or distracted. Make sure you both can focus. Begin by saying, "Is this a good time to talk about this?" If it is not, say, "When would be a better time?"

Fight about the Right Thing
If I were honest with myself, I would realize that many of the times I shout about things, it is not because of the immediate problem, but rather a bad day at work, or something someone else said, or a frustration with a man or machine that I am simply taking out on the easiest target.

It's also a good idea to avoid small arguments on days when, for example, daddy lost his job, mommy broke her toe, or Junior brought home F's on his report card.

Fight at the Right Intensity
The wildest argument my wife and I ever got into was over a baked potato. The second-most was over a tiny gash above my eyebrow. Now, obviously there were other serious issues involved, but the straws that broke the camel's back were the cut and the potato. This prevented us, for days, from seeing the real issues at hand and dealing with them in a godly way.

Never use violence. It is not a cause for divorce, but it sure is a cause for calling the police. Such an altercation will ruin your reputation in the community, will result in all kinds of unwanted attention from the authorities, will incur huge expenses, will often result in the loss of a job, and will make matters much worse.

Avoid insults. It is ok to say, "I don't like it when dirty laundry is all over the house. It makes me nervous that someone will knock on the door and want to come in. And it makes me distracted and annoyed when I'm home. What can we do?" It is not ok to say, "You are such a filthy slob!"

It is ok to say, "I am worried that if you do not find a job, we won't be able to make it through the next six months. What can we do?" It is not ok to say, "You are a lazy bum!"

It is okay to say, "I feel like I'm always correcting and spanking the kids, and you are ignoring their bad behavior. What can we do?" It is not ok to say, "You are a spineless wimp, just like your father was!"

One cutting insult causes wounds that are very difficult to erase, even with flowers and a countless compliments and reassurances. Some insults, once spoken, can never be fully erased. See to it that you do not speak them. Solomon says, "Death and life are in the power of the tongue ..." (Proverbs 18:21) and "there is one who speaks rashly like the thrusts of a sword ..." (12:18). Proverbs 15:1 says, "... a harsh word stirs up anger."

Fully and Freely Forgive
Do not commit emotional blackmail. Once you have granted forgiveness for a past sin, you give up your right to hold it against the other person. You aren't allowed to bring it up again to gain an advantage. For example, I know a wife who forgave her husband for committing adultery, but from then on, whenever he resisted buying a big-ticket item like a new car, jewelry, or a fancy vacation, he would hear, "Don't you remember what you did to me? I think I deserve this!" That's not forgiveness.

Now, it's a good idea to learn from past mistakes. She might remind him to stay out of certain situations that led to disaster in the past if she sees him treading on dangerous ground. But she ought not use it as blackmail. Ephesians 4:32 says, "Be kind to one another, tender-hearted, forgiving each other, just as God in Christ has forgiven you."

May we learn to address our complaints in a reasonable, loving, and God-honoring way. Nabal and Abigail show us marriage at its worst. While in most relationships both spouses shoulder at least some of the blame for a rotten marriage, sadly it seems Abigail just drew the short straw. Maybe this is why God rescued her in such a startling fashion. In any case, let us labor to be sure that we do better for one another.

How to Fight So You Both Win

Readings:
- The story of Abagail and Nabal in 1 Samuel 25:2–42
- Paul's description of Christian conflict resolution in Ephesians 4:22–32

Prep questions:
1. How does poor communication doom many marriages?

2. How can couples use words, or the lack thereof, to punish? Why is this a terrible idea?

3. What are some practical ways couples can arrange to communicate so that they will attack the problem rather than each other?

4. Why is it so important to practice forgiveness? What does real forgiveness require?

Chapter Six

Abraham & Sarah:
"She Called Him Lord"
The Gift of Submission

It's hard to find a more unpopular doctrine these days than male leadership of the home and church. But, if we take the Bible at its word, God has made the husband the head of the household.

> Christ is the head of every man, and the man is the head of a woman, and God is the head of Christ (1 Corinthians 11:3).

Carefully notice that this passage does not assert male leadership over any and every woman, but strictly over his wife. The challenge is to distinguish between what God expects of biblical couples, and the way submission is often caricatured in modern society. We must figure out what submission means, and what it does not mean.

Not Paul's Idea. God's!
Some suggest that first-century Bible writers were products of a misogynistic society, and echoed those thoughts in their letters to churches. Since our culture has progressed beyond this view, the argument is that we Christians are free to define the husband and wife relationship in different ways. That Peter and Paul have no special authority to declare what works best in the home.

There are two problems with this suggestion. First, it is impossible to be true to God without being true to His word. We cannot fairly approach the Bible as a smorgasbord, heaping our plate with desserts, and avoiding veggies. One must never add to nor take away from His inspired word (Revelation 22:18–19; Deuteronomy 4:2). If we trust God, we will understand that His will is designed to make the best of the human condition, not to make it intolerable. There are things in God's will that I don't completely understand, or sometimes (if I may speak carefully) don't agree with. That is, if I were making the rules, I would have made them differently. But I recognize that I am not the one making the rules, that God is more capable and qualified. I confess that God is righteous. I admit that His commandments are never burdensome and are for my good. The same God who wrote John 3:16 wrote 1 Corinthians 11:3. Like any child dealing with his father, there are bound to be times when I must simply obey first, and get the answers to my questions later. I trust that I will understand God's rules more completely in the end.

Second, Paul does not base these admonitions on his own supposed misogyny, or on his Jewish or Roman or Greek social background, but rather on God's work in Genesis. Here is what he says about women's role in the church:

> A woman must quietly receive instruction with entire submissiveness. But I do not allow a woman to teach or exercise authority over a man, but to remain quiet. For it was Adam who was first created, and then Eve. And it was not Adam who was deceived, but the woman being deceived fell into transgression. But women will be preserved through the bearing of children if they continue in faith and love and sanctity with self-restraint (1 Timothy 2:11–15).

The word here "quiet" (in KJV, "silent") does not indicate an absence of sound, but rather a tranquil and respectful demeanor (compare the use of the same word of men in 2 Thessalonians 3:12).

Paul says submission comes because of the order of creation, and as a consequence of the fall of mankind in Eden, where Eve's actions caused God to declare that her husband "shall rule over you" (3:16). We may not fully understand this arrangement, but we can't blame Paul for it. He was declaring what God gave him. Creation established two different but equally important spheres which the sexes were equipped to handle.

This is why congregations that are striving to stay true to the Scripture do not allow women to teach adult Bible classes or lead in worship. Not because they aren't capable—many could do a better job! But because this is the arrangement God ordained in the Garden of Eden, and revealed to disciples of all ages through the inspiration of the word.

Not Taken. Only Given!
It is important to understand that submission is a gift that must be given. It can never be taken, certainly not by force. Not only is the use of physical force an ungodly way for a husband to treat his wife, but it is no longer the definition of submission.

Let me illustrate: If a police officer pulls over a driver and asks him to step out of his car, submission to authority requires the driver to step out politely. If the driver refuses, and the officer is forced to grab him by the collar and haul him out the open window, the same end result is achieved, but the relationship is no longer one of submission. Submission can never be taken, only given.

Peter provides a much longer treatment of this subject in a discussion of the relationship of Abraham and Sarah.

> In the same way, you wives be submissive to your husbands so that even if any of them are disobedient to the word, they may be won without a word by the behavior of their wives, as they observe your chaste and respectful behavior. Your adornment must not be merely external—braiding the hair, and wearing gold jewelry, or putting on dresses; but let it be the hidden person of the heart, with the imperishable quality of a gentle and quiet spirit, which is precious in the sight of God. For in this way in former times the holy women also, who hoped in God, used to adorn themselves, being submissive to their own husbands; just as Sarah obeyed Abraham, calling him lord, and you have become her children if you do what is right, without being frightened by any fear. You husbands in the same way, live with your wives in an understanding way, as with someone weaker, since she is a woman; and show her honor as a fellow heir of the grace of life, so that your prayers will not be hindered (1 Peter 3:1–7).

Submission does not indicate inferiority. Peter is careful to state that women are spiritually equal, "joint heirs" of salvation (see also Galatians 3:28). There are many relationships in the Bible and in life where submission is required. Jesus submitted to His parents, and they were not superior to Him (Luke 2:51). Citizens are to be subject to government authorities (Romans 13:1), regardless of whether the officers with the badges are faster, smarter, or stronger. Church members are to be subject to elders (Hebrews 13:17; 1 Peter 5:5) as a result of their God-given office, not as a result of their level of education or wealth.

Clearly, in our modern American society, Sarah would not be looked up to as a hero for calling her husband lord. But God holds her forth as an example to emulate. I'm not sure that there is one specific incident that Peter is referring to (though a similar phrase is found in Genesis 18:12). But, there were many times in Sarah's life where she had to dutifully follow her husband's calling to pursue God's wishes. She embodied an overall pattern of submitting to his will, as he submitted to God's will. When Abraham left Ur of the Chaldees and began walking west "to a land which I will show you" (Genesis 12:1), Sarah would no doubt have been upset to leave the comforts of home and family, facing a hard, unsettled life.

This is not to say that Abraham was perfect; sometimes his leadership was wrong (Genesis 20:2). Wives do not follow the leadership of husbands because they are always correct, but because they endeavor to ascertain God's will for the family, and carry it out humbly. As such, God took good care of Sarah and kept His promises, and she became the mother of all the faithful.

Not Relaxation. Responsibility!
Too many modern women formed their ideas of submission in marriage by watching lazy fathers lay around, make bossy demands, refuse to touch "women's work," and domineer their wives or worse. Biblical submission is caricatured as the husband reclining in his boxer shorts, flipping through channels, and hollering to his wife to bring him another drink before she hurries and finishes dinner. If bowing to his every selfish whim is what submission in marriage is all about, then I fully understand why women would desire to be freed from it.

This is not, however, the relationship that the Bible envisions. Peter has a message for husbands, too; to live with her "in an understanding way" and to grant her the "honor" which she deserves as a fellow object of God's love.

Maybe the best description of the roles of husbands and wives is found in Ephesians 5:22–33. It says that wives must submit to and respect their husbands. But it also says that husbands must love and cherish and lead their wives.

> Wives, be subject to your own husbands, as to the Lord. For the husband is the head of the wife, as Christ also is the head of the church, He Himself being the Savior of the body. But as the church is subject to Christ, so also the wives ought to be to their husbands in everything. Husbands, love your wives, just as Christ also loved the church and gave Himself up for her.

The leadership and submission Paul describes is a relationship in which the husband makes decisions that are designed to selflessly provide the best things for his family, and ultimately steer them toward heaven. There is authority there, to be sure. The final decision rests with the husband. The blame for bad decisions rests with the husband. But he is supposed to use his leadership selflessly, to do what's best for his family, just as Christ sacrificed His own desires to nourish the church.

Perhaps a real-world example will help envision it. Dad might call a family meeting and say, "Winter break is coming up, and it looks like we will have two weeks off at the same time. Where would you all like to go on vacation?" He might even start the discussion, "We visited my parents last year, so honey we could visit your folks this year (even if, deep down, he cringes at the thought, he knows it's important to her, and fair). Or, maybe you have other ideas?"

She and the kids might say, "We've always wanted to take that ski vacation. Let's do it this year!" Now, dad might hate snow. He might have his heart set on sand and sunshine. But he is going to selflessly put his desires on hold and do everything within his power to accommodate his family. He will listen to them, and they will never feel afraid to communicate. He will weigh their desires respectfully and lovingly.

But dad might also say, "No." He might do a little research, and discover that even a basic ski vacation is going to cost over $10,000 in airfare, car, lodging, equipment rental, and food, and determine that there is no way the family can afford that. They may beg and plead! But this is where leadership has to come in and say, "We just can't afford that. I would love for us to be able to do that together! We could put it on credit cards, but that would cause us all sorts of trouble down the road." And that's when the family has to defer to his leadership. God has given him the responsibility to make that decision—not to make him feel puffed up—but to direct the family in a godly way.

He might also immediately say, "I'll tell you what. Let's go on a cheap vacation this year. We will save some money there, and we will put aside an additional $1,000 a month all year long. And then next year, even though it's not my favorite thing in the world, we will go on a great ski vacation." Or, it may be that mom comes up with that idea, and Dad says, "That's a great idea! What she said!" A real leader is not threatened when other members of the team get the credit for great ideas. His goal is simply to build up a loving, heaven-bound family.

So, husbands, when it comes to matters of family leadership, God has made you the captain. Don't foist the blame of family failure on your wife or children. It rests with you. Lead in such a way that is selfless, putting the needs of your family first. Lead in such a way that generates love and respect rather than resentment or even fear. Communicate and care. Protect your family from burdens that they ought not have to bear, because it's your responsibility to bear them. Be mindful that the wants of the family might occasionally run counter to what Christ wants for your family. Boldly say, "Our family is not going to see that movie, no matter how badly you want to go," or to say "We are not buying that car no matter how much you want it," or "I know that party seems important but it's not important enough to skip church." Husbands will be called into judgment for their shepherding of the family (Romans 14:12)!

Abraham didn't lead Sarah out of Ur of the Chaldees because he wanted to be closer to a golf course. He did so to save the family from spiritual trouble and to follow God's plan for his life. He had the best interests of his home in mind the entire time. Sarah deferred to his leadership, and God blessed the world as a result.

Not to Belittle Women. To Honor!
A husband and wife working together to fit this pattern will find smooth sailing. When this is the kind of selfless leadership shown by a godly husband, most women are happy to submit to it. They feel liberated and appreciated. They understand that God has placed her on a pedestal in the home, and freed her from responsibilities she does not wish to bear, allowing her to fully become the woman she wants to be. In fact, many godly women *resent* having to lead in place of their husbands.

The Bible greatly uplifts the role of women in the church. Only the misguided accuse the Bible of being anti-woman. It is certainly true that the New Testament places some restrictions on the role of women in public worship assemblies (1 Timothy 2:11–12) and that these chafe modern sensibilities.

Throughout the New Testament, women are vital to the function of the church, and are equally busy about the spread of God's kingdom. There is more to a strong congregation than a worship service. In the New Testament, we often see women active in these areas.

Women are especially vital to the comforting and helping ministries of the church (Acts 9:36–39). Paul praised those women who have,

> a reputation for good works; and if she has brought up children, if she has shown hospitality to strangers, if she has washed the saints' feet, if she has assisted those in distress, and if she has devoted herself to every good work (1 Timothy 5:9–10).

Now, it's not always thrilling to be involved in cooking, sewing, cleaning, and dealing with rugrats. First of all, don't knock the tremendous worth and value of these things; the hand that rocks the cradle rules the world, and women excel in that sphere. The church suffers when they are not provided. Families suffer when her great contributions are not appreciated (Proverbs 31:28).

But, these are not the only things we find women doing. Lydia the businesswoman opened her home to give the traveling evangelists a base of operations (Acts 16:15). Chloe was a concerned member of the Corinthian church (1 Corinthians 1:11). Phoebe was a standout servant of the church in Cenchrea (Romans 16:1). Indeed, time would fail to recount all the amazing and vital contributions of women in the Bible and in the modern kingdom of God.

The Gift of Submission

Readings:
- Peter's comments on Abraham and Sarah in 1 Peter 3:1–5
- Paul's description of marriage in Ephesians 5:22–33

Prep questions:

1. What are your own personal feelings about submission and leadership in marriage? What forces are responsible for forming these feelings?

2. What is the definition of submission in marriage?

3. What are some of the practical results of obeying God's commandments regarding submission? Of disobeying?

4. Think of one situation in your marriage, or someone else's, which illustrates how a dilemma was handled through submission. What worked? What could have been handled better?

Chapter Seven

The Shulammite Girl and Her Shepherd Boy: Marriage and Sexuality

So far, I have presented couples from the Bible to demonstrate what a noble, meaningful, beautiful, and deep responsibility is involved in the marriage relationship. But on our wedding night, I wasn't thinking about our financial future, our responsibilities as spouses, or what a team for Christ we would be. No, I was thinking about how fast we could ditch our families and the crowd of well-wishers, how far over the speed limit I could drive to the hotel without getting pulled over, and how quickly I could make the elevator lift us to the honeymoon suite!

Many times, Christians take a rather prudish view toward sexual intimacy. But we must realize that an entire book of the Bible is devoted to the subject.

Reading the Song of Solomon aloud will make you blush! In fact, not so very long ago it was taboo to read passages from the Song in a mixed audience. Many commentators could not accept that the inspired word would give so much attention to physical intimacy, so they treated it as an allegory of Christ's love for the church. Beautiful hymns such as *Jesus, Rose of Sharon* and *The Lily of the Valley,* were written from this perspective (2:1). The Puritans labored to find ways to make her lips (4:11) the word of God, and her navel (7:2) a baptistery.

While marital bliss is in many ways an illustration of Christ's love for the church, there are very good reasons to reject the allegorical view of the Song. First of all, while the Bible is full of literary devices such as symbolism and metaphor, allegory is generally recognized as later invention. Allegory verges on the anti-historical, and does not seem appropriate in Scripture, save for the brief parables of Christ. Nor would the Song be complete as an allegory—because the greatest expression of Christ's love for the church was His sacrifice, and that doesn't make an appearance in the Song at all. In fact, no New Testament writer quotes from the Song as an example of Christ's love for the church. Furthermore, there are candid descriptions of sexuality (Genesis 1:28) and sensuality elsewhere in Scripture (Proverbs 5:15–20). As a vital human experience, it seems entirely worthy to devote 117 verses to love and marriage. Finally, G. Lloyd Carr in his Tyndale series commentary shows that the Song of Solomon shares many important similarities with (and meaningful differences from) contemporary love poems in the ancient near East. I am convinced the Song of Solomon was written to celebrate intimacy in marriage.

There are a handful of competing theories about the number and identity of speakers, but it seems best to me to understand the Song of Solomon as describing a young Shulammite girl who has fallen in love with a shepherd boy. Some outside forces, including social standing, time, and distance (and, according to some interpretations, the unwelcome intrusion of King Solomon) make it difficult for them to be together, but they overcome these forces and finally join together in marriage, with the support of the whole community. There are elaborate, poetic, sensual descriptions of the body and of sexual activity. The Song of Solomon is a tribute to what is, for most people, the most electrifying human experience this side of heaven.

And yet, sexuality as God designed and exhibited in the Song is a bit different from sexuality as often depicted on movie screens.

Sex Is a Beautiful Gift of God
Clearly, God does not suggest that we take a prudish view toward sexual intimacy. God created the human body (Genesis 2:24–25) with all its working parts, and said "they shall become one flesh." Sex is not vulgar. Wanting sex does not indicate a dirty mind. Paul says that "men who forbid marriage and advocate abstaining from foods" are teaching evil doctrines, for God has created these things "to be gratefully shared in by those who believe and know the truth" (1 Timothy 4:1–4). Therefore, God says,

> Let your fountain be blessed,
> And rejoice in the wife of your youth.
> As a loving hind and a graceful doe,
> Let her breasts satisfy you at all times;
> Be exhilarated always with her love (Proverbs 5:18–19).

Sexual intimacy is nothing to be ashamed of. It is to be taught, anticipated, celebrated, and enjoyed.

There is an unwritten theory that men enjoy sex and women only tolerate it. That's not at all true. The Apostle Paul points out in 1 Corinthians 7:2–3, "Because of immoralities, let each man have his own wife, and let each woman have her own husband. Let the husband fulfill his duty to his wife, and likewise also the wife to her husband." A man who treats his wife in a demeaning way is failing to honor her. A man who is concerned only for his own pleasure and not his wife's pleasure is not living selflessly as a Christian should.

In the Song of Solomon, both the shepherd boy and the Shulammite girl look forward to whole-heartedly participating in the sexual union. Indeed, she speaks considerably more lines than he does! She twice says, "I am lovesick. Let his left hand be under my head, and his right hand embrace me" (2:5–6; 8:3).

To sample how exciting and breathtaking sexual intimacy is supposed to be, we can just read a few passages. The shepherd boy says to her,

> How beautiful you are, my darling,
> How beautiful you are!
> Your eyes are like doves behind your veil;
> Your hair is like a flock of goats
> That have descended from Mount Gilead …
> Your lips are like a scarlet thread,
> And your mouth is lovely …
> You are altogether beautiful my darling,
> And there is no blemish in you.
> Come with me from Lebanon, my bride …
> You have made my heart beat faster, my sister, my bride;
> You have made my heart beat faster with a single glance of your eyes,
> With a single strand of your necklace (4:1–9).

He goes on to praise every inch of her form in rich detail. She does the same, picking up the description.

> My beloved is dazzling and ruddy,
> Outstanding among ten thousand.
> His head is like gold, pure gold;
> His locks are like clusters of dates
> And black as a raven … (5:10–16).

And she, too, goes on for line after line, praising every inch of his form. Together, they describe their longing for one another. The shepherd boy begins,

> How beautiful and how delightful you are,
> My love, with all your charms!

> Your stature is like a palm tree,
> And your breasts are like its clusters.
> I said, "I will climb the palm tree,
> I will take hold of its fruit stalks."
> O may your breasts be like clusters of the vine,
> And the fragrance of your breath like apples,
> And your mouth like the best wine!

And she continues right where he left off.

> It goes down smoothly for my beloved,
> Flowing gently through the lips of those who fall asleep.
> I am my beloved's,
> And his desire is for me.
> Come, my beloved, let us go out into the country,
> Let us spend the night in the villages.
> Let us rise early and go to the vineyards;
> Let us see whether the vine has budded
> And its blossoms have opened,
> And whether the pomegranates have bloomed.
> There I will give you my love (7:6–12).

Such a scene is as innocent and beautiful as Adam and Eve living in Paradise. The longer we can hold on to such powerful experiences, the closer we are to God's intention for our lives.

God Designed Sex for Marriage

This passionate longing between the Shulammite girl and her shepherd boy is very healthy and wonderful. But God is not inviting us to take a permissive view toward sexual intimacy. This is not an invitation toward a 60's love-in, or a modern one-night stand. God created sexuality to be enjoyed, but He created the marriage relationship, and designated that devoted and selfless union as the best and only environment for expressing sexuality.

Every time the Bible mentions sexual intimacy outside the boundaries of a committed marriage, problems arise. Judah had sex with Tamar (Genesis 38), and she used his indiscretion to bribe him; his weakness also earned his father's scorn. Eli's sons slept with the women of the tabernacle (1 Samuel 2), and God was so offended at the impropriety that he destroyed them; it's one of the few times in the Bible where it so plainly says, "the Lord desired to put them to death." David ruined not only his own life, but his children's lives, and the lives of many in his kingdom for generations to come, because he took Bathsheba (2 Samuel 11). Amnon lured Tamar into his bedroom (2 Samuel 13), which led to his own murder at the hands of her angry brother.

Sex outside of marriage has physical consequences and emotional consequences. And despite anecdotes that living together before marriage ensures a couple's compatibility, many surveys show that couples who cohabitate go on to divorce at a significantly higher rate than couples who do not (Dr. Kevan Leman, *Sheet Music,* p. 18). If a couple doesn't fall in love without sex, they may discover that they are building their relationship on something less than God designed. Sex creates very powerful feelings, which can complicate a casual relationship, but which can tightly bind together a holy marriage relationship.

Even if scientific advances perfectly guard against all the problems associated with premarital sex—venereal disease and unplanned pregnancy; even if social changes perfectly smooth over all the emotional stigmas associated with premarital sex, there are still spiritual consequences. God prohibits adultery and fornication, and says that they will keep a person out of heaven. "Or do you not know that the unrighteous shall not inherit the kingdom of God? Do not be deceived; neither fornicators, nor idolaters, nor adulterers ... will inherit the kingdom of God" (1 Corinthians 6:9–10). "Marriage is to be held in honor among all, and the marriage bed is to be undefiled; for fornicators and adulterers God will judge" (Hebrews 13:4). God doesn't lay down these rules to be a killjoy, but rather to increase our happiness!

The Song of Solomon upholds this ethic as well. Repeatedly, the Shulammite girl says,

> I adjure you, O daughters of Jerusalem,
> By the gazelles or by the hinds of the field,
> That you do not arouse or awaken my love
> Until she pleases (2:7; 3:5; 8:4; *cf* 4:12; 7:13; 8:9–12).

Her frank descriptions of longing prove that she was really looking forward to their sexual union. But until the nuptial feast, she was "a locked garden" (4:12). Her "choice fruits" she had "saved up for you, my beloved" (7:13). Sexual intimacy is supposed to be exciting and breathtaking. But it is also supposed to be pure and innocent. Virginity is the best gift a husband or wife can give to their spouse on their wedding night.

Sex Is Only One Component of a Great Marriage

While it never takes the place of good communication and selfless love, sexual intimacy is a large component of a happy and successful marriage.

The shepherd boy does not look at the Shulammite girl as a brainless sex object. He calls her, "my sister, my bride." (4:10). In fact, this is one of my favorite examples of what a great marriage can be today, and why it is important to seek a Christian spouse—wouldn't we want a lifetime companion who not only excites us physically, but who treats us as a brother or sister in Christ?

On her part, she does not allow his muscular frame overshadow her attraction to his personality. She calls him, "my beloved" (4:16) and "my friend" (5:16). She praises not only his form, but his provision for her (1:16–17). She is as interested in his name (1:3) as his body.

They both know that there are many other potential partners in the world, but they are the only ones in each other's eyes (1:8; 5:2; 5:10). He says to her, "there are sixty queens and eighty concubines, and maidens without number; but my dove, my perfect one, is unique" (6:8–9).

Couples who love one another in the bedroom are constantly building each other up. Sexual intimacy makes the marriage stronger. Intimacy, while it doesn't fix problems, can provide a welcome rest from the stresses of life. Couples who are passionately in love usually find that it is an exciting, though minor, part of their already-wonderful relationship. Couples who withhold sex, or who allow no more than occasional begrudging consent, often find that sex is a huge part of their relationship—a very negative part.

Practically speaking, a couple should buy locks for the doors to ensure privacy, learn to go to bed together at the same time, carve out time in their hectic lives for each other, continue to date one another actively, take weekends away, enforce a consistent early bedtime for the children, practice good hygiene, and most of all, be romantic (which is defined as affection not necessarily leading to the bedroom—such as giving flowers for no reason, going out to dinner, helping with chores, holding hands, or writing a nice note). It is said that a husband who wants his wife to love him in the bedroom must first pay attention to her in the living room and kitchen. A husband who is affectionate, helpful, and kind, who "nourishes and cherishes" his wife (Ephesians 5:29), usually has a wife who is excited to participate in intimacy.

Thus, the Song of Solomon is much, much more than a paperback romance novel. There are many other aspects of their relationship. In short, the church has a huge stake in mentoring young couples, encouraging young love within the church, and instructing what to look for in a mate.

The Shulammite girl and her shepherd boy show us the adventurous delight of young, committed love. Their relationship encourages us to recapture that same degree of devotion and willingness to fight for one another, as we had when we first got married. God invites us—"drink and imbibe deeply, O lovers" (5:1)! This is one exciting way in which marriage allows us to express our love for one another.

> Many waters cannot quench love,
> Nor will rivers overflow it;
> If a man were to give all the riches of his house for love,
> It would be utterly despised (8:7).

Marriage and Sexuality

Readings:
- The love story in Song of Solomon 4–7; better yet, just read the whole thing

Prep questions:
1. Why do some people suggest that sex is dirty?

2. Why is sex holy in a marriage relationship, but nowhere else?

3. What are some common myths people have regarding sex? What are the sources of these myths?

4. What is one practical way to ensure that sex is part of a greater marriage relationship?

Chapter Eight

David & Bathsheba: Protecting Your Marriage

David messed up. The man after God's own heart totally, royally messed up.

One day David had nothing to do. His kingdom was secure. His palace was finished. Joab and his soldiers were fighting the Ammonites and besieging the city of Rammah. But David stayed home.

> When evening came, David arose from his bed and walked around on the roof of the king's house, and from the roof he saw a woman bathing; and the woman was very beautiful in appearance. So David sent and inquired about the woman. And one said, "Is this not Bathsheba, the daughter of Eliam, the wife of Uriah the Hittite?" (2 Samuel 11:2–3).

Some sins appear in our pathways suddenly, like potholes in the road that we must swerve to avoid. David didn't sin when he caught a glance of Bathsheba down below the palace walls. David could have let it drop, or better yet, sent a servant to ensure that Bathsheba moved her tub. David could have been thankful for the many other wives living with him in the palace below. But David took a dangerous step of inquiring about her.

When he discovered that she was "the wife of Uriah," that should have been the end of it. David had multiple opportunities to abandon his course of action that was hurtling inevitably toward sin. He did not have to contact her further, but "David sent messengers and took her" (v. 4). David could have had an innocent conversation with her in the openness of the palace corridors, but David "lay with her." Really, once Bathsheba was invited into his home, the result was a foregone conclusion.

Perhaps David thought this was the end of the matter. She returned to her house and David turned his attention to other things. But within a few weeks, "she sent and told David, and said, 'I am pregnant'" (v. 5). This is where the panic and conniving began. David instructed Joab to send Uriah home from the war, on a pretense of needing information. But he was really trying to get Uriah to spend the night with his wife Bathsheba. If he hurried, Bathsheba's pregnancy could be reasonably credited to Uriah. But Uriah was very conscientious about the fact that his fellow soldiers and his commanders were camping in the open field without the comforts of home. His righteous thoughts were focused on the Ark of the Covenant, the presence of God at the battlefront. He decided not to go to his house and his wife, but rather slept on the ground with the servants. David tried with assurances, with gifts, and with liquor to convince Uriah to go home, but he steadfastly stayed in the servants' quarters. David needed another plan.

He drafted a letter and sealed it and instructed Uriah himself to deliver it to Joab. With sad irony, David could trust Uriah not to look inside. It was his own death sentence, which David intended to carry out sneakily. He instructed Joab to put Uriah in the hottest part of the battle and then withdraw, to let him be killed. The strategy worked, and Joab sent to David a coded message that Uriah was dead.

David decided the coast was clear. "...David sent and brought her to his house and she became his wife; then she bore him a son." David probably thought he had a brush with disaster, but through wise and careful handling, he had gotten away with it. Things settled down, and months went by, and Bathsheba gave birth to a healthy son. However, the chapter ends with these ominous words: "But the thing that David had done was evil in the sight of the Lord" (v. 27).

The prophet Nathan surprised David, and confronted him with his own sin. He accused him of thanklessness, of faithlessness, of adultery, and murder. David humbled himself and repented, and begged forgiveness, and God forgave his sin (12:13). But the consequences of this action would haunt David forever. God said, "the sword shall never depart from your house" (v. 10), and "I will raise up evil against you from your own household" (v. 11). God decreed that David would suffer shame not secretly but in broad daylight (v. 12), and that God would take the life of the young child (v. 14). David prayed for God to change His mind, but He would not. Perhaps the loss of the child was the most proximate and obvious punishment. But in reality, worse was yet to come. For as a result of David's indiscretion, the rest of his life was filled with political intrigue and backstabbing. His son Absalom rebelled against him, forcing David to flee for a time, and causing his wives and children to suffer. Other sons raised their hands against him and tried to overthrow him. And even though God kept His promises to David and considered him a paragon of faithfulness, David's reputation took a hit that he would never fully live down. Even though people will always remember

David as a great leader and a man after God's own heart, they will also hasten to add, "except in the case of Uriah the Hittite" (1 Kings 15:5).

Avoid Adultery at All Costs
Yes, adultery is that bad. Nothing will destroy a ministry, a family, or a marriage with the same terrible efficiency as adultery. Esau gave up his birthright for a bowl of stew; some people give up their marriage, their most loyal companion, their home, their financial security, and their children, for a moment's indiscretion.

Most of the first nine chapters of Proverbs represent Solomon's advice to his own son. Of 249 verses (Proverbs 1:8–9:18), a full 66 verses, or 27%, discuss the dangers and consequences of sexual immorality (see 5:1–23; 6:20–35; 7:1–27). Obviously, it's a big deal, something to be avoided at all costs.

Solomon's words of warning can be boiled down to a simple phrase: "It is not worth it!" The moment of careless passion will soon be replaced by a long period of pain and anguish, possibly even a lifetime of regret. Solomon says, "For the lips of an adulteress drip honey and smoother than oil is her speech; but in the end she is bitter as wormwood, sharp as a two-edged sword. Her feet go down to death, her steps lay hold of Sheol" (Proverbs 5:3–5). "Do not desire her beauty in your heart, nor let her capture you with her eyelids. For on account of a harlot one is reduced to a loaf of bread..." (Proverbs 6:25–26).

Pre-Adultery Checklist
It is important to inoculate ourselves against sin during a time of strength, so that we will not fall victim in a time of weakness. Solomon urged his son to bind his godly teachings on his heart in a day of calm reflection (Proverbs 6:20–24), so that they would already be in place to provide guidance and protection in a day of quick decision. The time to learn God's word is not during a crisis. Our senses must be trained to discern good and evil (Hebrews 5:14) long before we find ourselves faced with sin. There's not a person who can call time out and suggest a little Bible study when already in the backseat! You need to already be convinced. You need to already know what you will say and do.

One of my most valuable lists is a series of thoughts that one should consider *before* making the decision to sin. While these thoughts are helpful before any type of sin, I sometimes have labeled it my "pre-adultery checklist."

- Think: sin looks good and feels good for a moment, but it will have painful physical and spiritual consequences (Galatians 6:7–8).
- Think: sin would be a slap in the face of my Savior, who gave His life to free me from sin (Hebrews 6:4–6).
- Think: sin invokes the wrath of God (1 Thessalonians 4:3–7; Hebrews 10:26–31). No activity, item, or relationship is worth spending an eternity in Hell (Mark 8:37; 9:43–48).
- Think: this sort of public sin will require confession for forgiveness. The thought of facing my family and my brethren and revealing my indiscretion is frightening. The thought of revealing my sins to the woman's husband is perhaps even worse (Proverbs 6:26–35).
- Think: sin would be a thankless rejection of the wonderful blessings God has already provided (Proverbs 5:15–20). I should count my blessings and focus on them.
- Think: sin is hypocrisy (Romans 2:22–24). It slanders God and destroys my ability to preach to others.
- Think: sin puts my companion in danger. I may find forgiveness, but he or she may not. Endangering her soul is not walking in love (1 John 2:10; 5:2–3).
- Think: sin may be committed where no one else sees, but God always sees (Hebrews 4:13).

Helpful Rules

Another way to be sure that the consequences of adultery never touch your home is to set rules with your spouse ahead of time, to ensure that you will not be tempted. While God promises to help us during times of temptation (1 Corinthians 10:13), sometimes the "way of escape" which He provides is found at an early point in the process. If you find yourself with someone in a hotel room in a distant city, do not blame God for tempting you beyond your ability to say no if you have failed to say no every step along the way.

Since a moment of weakness can ruin a family, a ministry, a life, it is important to keep the moment from coming in the first place. It is helpful to:

- Decide ahead of time that you will not meet with or travel with a person of the opposite sex. If such an appointment is unavoidable, always let your spouse know about it first, and have it in a public place.
- Keep no secrets from your spouse. Do not maintain hidden Facebook or email accounts. Have no passwords that your spouse doesn't have access to.

- Beware of flirting which starts innocently and escalates. Don't pay compliments that suggest interest. There is a difference between saying, "I really like your new hairdo," or, "That's a very nice outfit," and saying, "Wow, you look great in that outfit," or, "Where have you been all my life?"
- Most extra-marital affairs begin not with physical attraction but emotional connection. Invest emotion and time into your own marriage. "Drink water from your own cistern" (Proverbs 5:15).
- Beware of physical contact. Hugs and warm greetings are nice, but they can lead to other things. One handy rule is to do nothing that you wouldn't feel comfortable doing if your spouse were standing right behind you watching.
- Don't be naïve. Don't get into situations where you might have to turn summersaults to explain why things aren't how they appear. If you take care of how things look, you automatically take care of how things are. You will never have to explain yourself.
- Avoid all contact with anyone who makes your spouse nervous. For example, if you own a business and your new secretary makes your wife nervous, you must fire her. Also, do not attempt to contact old flames.
- Take steps to have pornography locked out. Keep computers in public areas of the home. Keep photos of your family on trips.

A Word about Pornography
Many people seem to think that pornography is a harmless pastime, a victimless crime. But in fact, it is responsible for destroying minds and homes. Even the worldly media is reporting the damage done by stumbling into internet porn, leading to a lifetime of emotional, social, and physical problems (see, for example, *Time* magazine, April 11, 2016).

Men who get involved in pornography learn to objectify women to such an extent that they find it increasingly difficult to relate to women as living, breathing, speaking, feeling people.

Spiritually, pornography is condemned. It is one of those works of the flesh like "immorality, impurity, sensuality" that sets its desire against the Spirit (Galatians 5:19). Jesus warns that "everyone who looks at a woman with lust" is playing with fire (Matthew 5:28). I have always appreciated how Job declared his righteousness, "I have made a covenant with my eyes; how then could I gaze at a virgin?" (Job 31:1). What goes in the eyes, which are "the lamp of the body" (Matthew 6:22–23), is a big part of how we shape our heart and our character; media choices are increasingly indicative of a person's relationship with God. I think it's a point of sensible pride when a Christian is asked, "Have you ever seen *Fifty Shades*?" to be able to honestly respond, "No way!"

Furthermore, couples must realize that viewing pornography together is neither helpful nor godly. Committing sin together doesn't magically make it righteous. Would it be ok, for example, to snort cocaine together in the privacy of your own living room? Couples certainly should date one another and spice up their relationship, but pornography is not the way to do it. Pornography actually drives you farther away from one another.

Realize that your marriage is the most important human relationship you have. Treasure it and guard it for all that you are worth! Statistics suggest that fidelity is increasingly uncommon. Truly, "many are the victims she [adulteress] has cast down, and numerous are all her slain" (Proverbs 7:26). See to it that your marriage is one of the strong and successful ones that escape her snares, and stands as an example to others.

Protecting Your Marriage

Readings:
- The story of David's great sin in 1 Samuel 11–12
- Solomon's advice to his son in Proverbs 5–7

Prep questions:
1. How many opportunities did David have to change course before engaging in adultery? What else did adultery lead him to do?

2. What is one of the practical consequences of adultery that Solomon mentions to his son?

3. Who is harmed by pornography?

4. How would you respond to someone who argued that setting rules is prudish and unnecessary?

Chapter Nine

Herod and Herodias:
The Tragedy of Divorce and Remarriage

The greatest prophet in the Bible was put to death because of his stand for the divine definition of marriage.

> For Herod himself had sent and had John arrested and bound in prison on account of Herodias, the wife of his brother Philip, because he had married her. For John had been saying to Herod, "It is not lawful for you to have your brother's wife." Herodias had a grudge against him and wanted to put him to death and could not do so, for Herod was afraid of John, knowing that he was a righteous and holy man, and he kept him safe ... (Mark 6:17–20).

A day came when, at a banquet, King Herod foolishly promised to give Herodias' daughter anything she wanted, and the girl's mother prompted her to ask for the head of John the Baptist. "And although the king was very sorry, yet because of his oaths and because of his dinner guests, he was unwilling to refuse her" (6:26).

Historians such as Josephus and Edersheim (*The Life and Times of Jesus the Messiah,* Book 3, chapter 28) tell us that a few years prior to these events, when Philip and his wife Herodias visited Philip's brother Herod in Judea, Herod took a liking to Herodias. He convinced her to divorce Philip and marry him instead. John the Baptist spoke out boldly against their union and flatly told Herod that it was not lawful for him to be married to Herodias.

Thus, we discover a startling biblical truth, that not all marriages recognized in the eyes of society are acceptable in the eyes of God.

Divorce
Statistics suggest that in the United States of America, around half of all marriages end in divorce. High profile couples split up for "irreconcilable differences." The standard of commitment used to be "until death do us part." Now it is "until we feel like a change."

Our human ways have gone so far astray from God's ways, it is vital to learn God's will regarding marriage, which He reveals in His word.

Matthew 19 is a good place to start:

> Some Pharisees came to Jesus, testing Him, and asking, "Is it lawful for a man to divorce his wife for any reason at all?"
>
> And He answered and said, "Have you not read that He who created them from the beginning made them male and female, and said, 'For this reason a man shall leave his father and mother and be joined to his wife, and the two shall become one flesh'? So they are no longer two, but one flesh. What therefore God has joined together, let no man separate."
>
> They said to Him, "Why then did Moses command to give her a certificate of divorce and send her away?"
>
> He said to them, "Because of your hardness of heart Moses permitted you to divorce your wives; but from the beginning it has not been this way. And I say to you, whoever divorces his wife, except for immorality, and marries another woman commits adultery."
>
> The disciples said to Him, "If the relationship of the man with his wife is like this, it is better not to marry."
>
> But He said to them, "Not all men can accept this statement, but only those to whom it has been given. For there are eunuchs who were born that way from their mother's womb; and there are eunuchs who were made eunuchs by men; and there are also eunuchs who made themselves eunuchs for the sake of the kingdom of heaven. He who is able to accept this, let him accept it" (Matthew 19:3–12).

Jesus makes it clear that, since creation, God's intention for marriage has been one man, one woman, for life. God reluctantly tolerated divorce for a time in the old covenant due to the hardness of the Jews' hearts; though there is a debate as to just what behaviors Moses permitted as grounds for divorce in Deuteronomy 24:1–4. Not many, it would seem, for the same God who inspired this passage said, "I hate divorce" (Malachi 2:13–16).

In any case, Jesus' teaching for the New Testament era is plain and incontrovertible. Jesus defines a second marriage as adultery. Now, adultery is not just common fornication; it is fornication when a marriage exists. The only way to make sense of this is that God views the first marriage as still in force. Again, "What God has joined together, let no man separate." Although the couple has divorced in civil court, Jesus speaks as if the marriage were intact. A man who divorces his wife and marries another woman commits adultery because and only because God still views him as married to his first wife.

If this sounds strict, it seems that the disciples also found Jesus' teaching shockingly inflexible. In fact, they immediately suggested that it might be better not to get married at all! Jesus did not attempt to alleviate their surprise, but replied that some found themselves in a situation where they had to remain celibate to be pleasing to God.

Other than death, Jesus provides only one exception to His prohibition on divorce and remarriage: "except for immorality" (see also Matthew 5:31-32). While "one man, one woman, for life" still best sums up God's plan for marriage, God permits a cheated-on person to put away his or her unfaithful spouse and be free to marry another. Actually, I would hope that such a couple would have the ability to forgive and repair the damage and remain together; but there are many situations where this is simply not possible (especially situations in which the behavior continues), and God recognizes that.

Other passages in the New Testament bear out Jesus' teaching on the indissolubility of marriage. In Romans 7:1–4, Paul uses the permanence of marriage to illustrate a point about the passing of the Law of Moses. He says,

> ...For the married woman is bound by law to her husband while he is living; but if her husband dies, she is released from the law concerning the husband. So then, if while her husband is living she is joined to another man, she shall be called an adulteress; but if her husband dies, she is free from the law, so that she is not an adulteress though she is joined to another man.

According to this text, if someone has a living spouse and marries another, he commits adultery. In 1 Corinthians 7:10–11, Paul says,

> But to the married I give instructions, not I, but the Lord, that the wife should not leave her husband (but if she does leave, she must remain unmarried, or else be reconciled to her husband), and that the husband should not divorce his wife.

Clearly, in the inspired words of Christ and Paul, God views some marriages as no marriage at all, but actually defines them as adultery. God's plan is that if a man and woman choose to marry, they remain faithful to one another for life. God Himself seals their vows in heaven, and He expects the promise to be maintained. Furthermore, God takes a dim view of that which He defines as adultery (1 Corinthians 6:9–10; Hebrews 13:4).

It is important for Christians to understand God's will on marriage and to communicate it to their families, to their congregations, and to the world. It is important to be faithful to our own vows and allow the power of commitment to keep us together through rough patches in our marriages. And it is extremely important to teach our children to choose a partner well, knowing that marriage is totally permanent. The church that spends more time teaching couples how to have a thrilling marriage relationship probably has to worry less about the consequences of divorce.

Some Difficult Implications

Because the divorce rate is so high, any disciple busy about the task of spreading the gospel sooner or later finds himself sitting across the kitchen table from a couple who are interested in the gospel, but who are in a marriage that Jesus defines as adultery. What does God require for repentance of this sin? That is perhaps the most uncomfortable, upsetting position an evangelist will ever find himself in. It is one of those times when the message of God feels less like good news and more like "the burden of the Lord" (Nahum 1:1). It is one of those times when the messenger must decide whether he will remain true to God, or "shrink from declaring the whole purpose of God" (Acts 20:27). It is one of those times when we must realize that it is our duty to be a faithful messenger rather than presumptuously claim the authority to legislate our own desires.

What does God require for repentance of this sin? Repentance is to have a change of heart regarding one's sin, and cease practicing it. If God defines a marriage as sinful, the only way to repent is to quit the marriage. It is horribly difficult to tell a couple they must separate to be saved—especially if they have a loving relationship and children. But, this doctrine is a "thus saith the Lord" and we must "speak the truth in love" (Ephesians 4:15).

I struggled with this mightily for many years—wrestling to reconcile the loving mercy of Jesus with the plain requirements of repentance. How could it be that a loving God would make a loving couple to separate in order to be saved? It seemed to me like correcting one wrong by committing another wrong. Then, one day, I ran across a passage deep in the book of Ezra. The standard of the Law is different here (marrying a foreigner rather than marrying a divorced individual) but the principle is clear.

> Shecaniah, the son of Jehiel, one of the sons of Elam, said to Ezra, "We have been unfaithful to our God and have married foreign

> women from the peoples of the land; yet now there is hope for Israel in spite of this. So now let us make a covenant with our God to put away all the wives and their children, according to the counsel of my lord and of those who tremble at the commandment of our God; and let it be done according to the law. Arise! For this matter is your responsibility, but we will be with you; be courageous and act." ... And some of them had wives by whom they had children (Ezra 10:2–4, 44).

If these Israelites wished to be right in His eyes, they needed to put away their illicit spouses. It was here that I learned that there are situations when a loving and merciful God would require a separation to become right in His eyes.

That doesn't mean declaring this truth is easy. Repentance for some is more difficult than for others. It can be heartbreaking. It made Herodias so angry she had the preacher killed. But the root of the problem is not in an uncompromising God who has declared His will regarding marriage commitment, but rather a drifting society that has redefined marriage as a contract of convenience, so that even good and honest people think nothing of dissolving it.

One foggy morning, a man and his friend went fishing on a local lake. The man fished from the dock, while the friend fished from a johnboat tied to the dock. The minds of both were lost in fishing, so that suddenly the friend looked up and realized he was fifty yards away from the man. He cried out, "Hey, what happened? How did you get way over there?" The man on shore replied, "Well, I'm pretty sure the dock didn't move; your line must have come off and you drifted!"

When people look up and notice a wide separation between society (including many church denominations) and the Bible, you can be assured it was society that drifted, not God. Most religious people agreed on this point 100 years ago. The tension regarding marriage and divorce in society is the fault of our modern age, not the fault of our holy God. So don't get angry at God—get angry at Satan!

What If the Couple Married Before Coming to Christ?

It does not matter if the marriage was entered before or after one became a Christian. God does not have one set of rules for Christians and one set of rules for non-Christians, but all shall be judged by His eternal word.

Baptism grants forgiveness of sin and entrance into the kingdom of God. It does not, however, change the nature of sins still being committed. Consider the example of a bank robber. He steals a million dollars, gets away with it, and buries it in his backyard. Later, he hears the gospel and genuinely wishes to repent and be saved. What is required for him to repent? Could he say, "I'm sorry I robbed the bank and I'll never do it again," receive baptism, and now unearth the money to spend it as he likes with a clean conscience? After all, the money was stolen before he was baptized, and he's been forgiven of the sin of stealing. Surely we can agree that baptism does not change the nature of the sin. If the converted bank robber spends the money or keeps it hidden, he perpetuates the sin. To repent, he must return the money and pay the consequences.

In the case of a marriage God defines as adultery, baptism can forgive sin, but it cannot change the nature of the marriage. God still defines the marriage as adultery. Repentance requires dissolving the union that Christ defines as adultery.

All fifty states recognize homosexual unions. If such a couple learned the gospel, and wanted to be saved, what would God require for repentance? Would baptism erase the sinful nature of their marriage, permitting them to remain in it? Certainly not. Would the church be correct to admonish them to separate, regardless of what the courts had recognized? Absolutely. Even if the church had to help care for the children involved.

This teaching may turn off many families to the gospel of Christ. But let not the church be discouraged. Nor let the members of the church ever fail to reach out to a family just because they are in a marriage that Jesus defines as adultery. Jesus' encounter with the Samaritan woman at the well (John 4:7-42) proves that those who have suffered divorce and those who are involved in sinful unions are deeply loved by God, and deserve a chance to hear the truth and repent and be saved. Jesus confronted her sin by saying, "you have had five husbands, and the one whom you now have is not your husband" (4:18), and yet, by the end of the conversation, she was telling everyone in the city that He was the Savior. Giving up one's spouse and living a celibate life may seem outrageously drastic, but there are some who have done just that. I know of no other way to understand it.

Conclusion

As Christians, we are called to "maintain these principles without favoritism, doing nothing in a spirit of partiality" (1 Timothy 5:21), even principles that we do not like. We must be careful lest we become like the false prophets of Jeremiah's day, of whom it is said,

> They heal the brokenness of the daughter of My people superficially, saying "Peace, peace!" But there is no peace (Jeremiah 8:11).

God is a loving and forgiving God. But he is also a God of truth and righteousness. God expresses love and grace in accordance with His word. If the God of truth and righteousness defines a certain type of marriage as adultery, and declares that people in adultery cannot go to heaven (1 Corinthians 6:9–10), it must be so. Thankfully, the same God of love and mercy has saved many people from an adulterous situation, for He says to the Corinthians,

> Such were some of you; but you were washed, but you were sanctified, but you were justified in the name of the Lord Jesus Christ and in the Spirit of our God (1 Corinthians 6:11).

God loved homosexuals and adulterers and everyone else so much He died on the cross to take away their sins. But He won't take them away unless they repent of them. Let us throw ourselves upon God's mercy in the way He prescribes.

And let us devote ourselves to choosing and becoming faithful spouses, so that we may live through the words of our commitment, "until death do us part."

The Tragedy of Divorce and Remarriage

Readings:
- Jesus' will regarding marriage and divorce in Matthew 19:1–12
- Paul's statements in 1 Corinthians 7:1–11

Prep questions:
1. Are God's will regarding marriage and society's rules regarding marriage the same?

2. What are some practical implications of Matthew 19:3–12?

3. Where should a couple's focus be to avoid having to think about divorce in the first place?

4. What does baptism change? What does baptism not change?

Chapter Ten

Hannah & Elkanah and Ruth & Boaz: My Spouse, My Greatest Encourager

The book of Samuel opens, not by introducing us to King David, or King Saul, or even the prophet Samuel, but to Samuel's mother Hannah.

When we first meet her, Hannah is childless. In the ancient world, a "barren womb" was a frustrating condition for a married woman. To make matters worse, she was not the only woman in the house. Her husband Elkanah had another wife, Peninah, who had children. In an act of inner-family bullying, Peninah, who is labeled as "a rival" in the text, "would provoke her bitterly to irritate her" (1:6) because of Hannah's childlessness.

I can easily imagine Elkanah piling on the abuse, or relegating her to a second-class status in the household, sending her to live in a shed on the back part of the property. But he did just the opposite. He saw her anguish, and treated her tenderly. When feast days would come, "to Hannah he would give a double-portion, for he loved Hannah" (1 Samuel 1:5).

It is touching that her husband Elkanah did what he could to make her feel special. There are many conditions and circumstances that will challenge a person's sense of self-confidence and diminish his or her will to get up and function. A husband may lose a job and enter a period of doubt, aimlessness, or depression. He may doubt his worth in society and in the home. A wife may have to take a regimen of chemotherapy and become weak, sick, and tired. She may not be able to keep the pace she once kept with a smile on her face.

It is in just such times that spouses can be the greatest source of encouragement. If it is a temporary setback, an encouraging spouse can help the struggling partner escape the sucking pull of the "woe is me" vortex, and regain feelings of worth and energy. If it is a permanent disability, spouses can improve what life is left.

See to it that your actions are designed to build up and meet the needs of your spouse. It is said that if a man looks forward to returning home to his wife, the Devil can't make the world bad enough to tear him down. He can face any stress at work, any disappointment, any opponent; he can crash the car and lose his job; he can break his leg and get a speeding ticket in a school zone; and yet if he can come home to a kind and loving wife, he can feel that all is right in his life, and rise the next morning ready and willing to meet the worst of the world once again.

This has less to do with providing the solution to every problem, and more to do with patience and understanding. Even Elkanah had difficulty understanding this. He, like most guys, wanted to fix the problem. He said, "Hannah, why do you weep and why do you not eat and why is your heart sad? Am I not better to you than ten sons?" (1:8). He certainly did his best! But there was nothing he could do to fill the hole in her heart; only make it more bearable. Thankfully, he kept building her up, never tearing her down. When she needed it, he gave her the space she required to seek God on her own terms (1:9–18).

Spouses are not always looking for fixes. Often, they just want a little understanding and patience. A supportive relationship at home makes up for the world's slights. "So Jacob served seven years for Rachel and they seemed to him but a few days because of his love for her" (Genesis 29:20). "Husbands, love your wives, and do not be embittered against them" (Colossians 3:19). "So husbands ought also to love their own wives as their own bodies. He who loves his own wife loves himself" (Ephesians 5:28). If you twist an ankle or break a finger, you protect it and baby it to give it a chance to heal. Do the same for each other. If one loses a job, help fill out new applications, and remind him how talented he is. If she is not feeling well, take up some of the slack around the house, cook some meals, do some dishes and laundry, and don't pout when she is not in the mood.

If it is a permanent change and no relief is on the horizon, an encouraging spouse can be there simply to provide comfort and lighten the load. If you face one of those tragic occurrences that cannot be fixed, make the problem the enemy, and not one another. It may not be fair, and it will never be easy. Who knows why the Lord allows some couples to go on cruises and exotic vacations long into their seventies, but shackles others a wheelchair distance from the house? But I have seen some of the greatest displays of love in devoted marriages going through tough times. A husband was diagnosed with cancer, and his wife took on a second job to make ends meet; she never berated him for his weakness. A wife suffered Alzheimer's, and the husband led her about by the hand and doted on her throughout a long five-year decline, and remained by her bedside until the very end. These acts of kindness and devotion make a very long list, and provide a wonderful example of what God designed marriage to provide in difficult circumstances.

Ekanah's encouragement continued even after the Lord answered Hannah's prayers. She had made a special vow to God in return for a son—that she would devote him to the tabernacle. When God provided a son, Elkanah was very understanding when she revealed that she needed to make good on her vow and drop off the boy forever. He said, "Do what seems best to you ... may the Lord confirm His word" (1 Samuel 1:23). According to the Law of Moses, he could have cancelled her vow (see Numbers 30). This kind of patience and trust is rare, and surely made her feel valued.

Proverbs 31:10–31 says, "An excellent wife, who can find? For her worth is far above jewels. The heart of her husband trusts in her, and he will have no lack of gain. She does him good and not evil all the days of her life...." Give each other the benefit of love and kindness each day, and you will have a glorious marriage.

The Character of Ruth
Selflessness and devotion during difficulty is featured at the center of another Bible story, the book of Ruth. These four little chapters are sandwiched between the dramatic actions of the Judges and the establishment of the kingdom in Samuel. It deserves its place, for it is a simple but powerful story of how kindness and loyalty can overcome almost any obstacle. Ruth's character was on display even before she became a wife to Boaz.

A family of Jews, Elimelech and his wife Naomi, and their two sons Mahlon and Chilion, left the territory of Israel to live in Moab. While there, the boys married Moabite women, Orpah and Ruth. At the end of a decade, all three men died, leaving Naomi, Orpah, and Ruth childless widows—one of the most destitute and desperate situations a woman could find herself in. Naomi made up her mind to return home, and encouraged her daughters-in-law to stay with their people and remarry, for they were young enough to start over again. Orpah wasted no time, and took off. But Ruth said,

> Do not urge me to leave you or turn back from following you; for where you go, I will go, and where you lodge, I will lodge. Your people shall be my people, and your God, my God (1:16).

Likely, in their decade together, Ruth had learned many things about the God of Israel, and was convinced that her idols had nothing to offer. But moreover, Ruth demonstrated selflessness, devotion, and service, in her willingness to endure the impoverished life of a widow in order to support her mother-in-law, rather than pursue her own happier course.

Her first humble task was to enter the fields during the barley harvest to glean (Leviticus 19:9–10); that is, to stoop and crawl through the already-harvested fields in order to locate grains that had been missed by the harvesters, to scrape together enough that she and Naomi could eat.

It wasn't exactly a glamorous lifestyle. But news of Ruth's selfless deeds spread throughout Bethlehem, Naomi's hometown. She happened to find herself in the field of Boaz, who was, it turned out, a relative of Naomi. Boaz encouraged her to stay in his fields, where she would be safe from uncouth servants. He ordered that she be given small kindnesses—drinks of water from the servants' rations, food from his table, and sheaves "accidentally" dropped in her path by the harvesters where she could easily gather them up. She wondered at these favors, and Boaz replied,

> All that you have done for your mother-in-law after the death of your husband has been fully reported to me, and how you left your father and your mother and the land of your birth, and came to a people that you did not previously know. May the Lord reward your work, and your wages be full from the Lord, the God of Israel, under whose wings you have come to take refuge (2:11–12).

Ruth continued to work all through the barley harvest. Naomi decided that God may have provided them an opportunity. Naomi encouraged her to make herself available to Boaz for marriage. That night, Ruth sought out Boaz's place and lay down at his feet. When he stirred, she said, "Spread your covering over your maid, for you are a close relative" (3:9). Interestingly, the word "covering" is exactly the same word as "wings" in 2:12. This was no shallow request for a warm blanket, but to be a part of the household of Boaz, and the household of God. Boaz replied,

> May you be blessed of the Lord, my daughter. You have shown your last kindness to be better than the first by not going after young men, whether poor or rich. Now, my daughter, do not fear. I will do for you whatever you ask, for all my people in the city know that you are a woman of excellence (3:10–11).

As a kinsman, he had the right to redeem what once belonged to Elimelech, Mahlon, and Chilion. This Boaz did, through legal means, and acquired Ruth as a wife at the same time.

Soon, Boaz and Ruth had a son, and the women said to Naomi,

> Blessed is the Lord who has not left you without a redeemer today, and may his name become famous in Israel. ...for your daughter-in-law, who loves you and is better to you than seven sons, has given birth to him (4:14–15).

And—here is the most interesting part of the story—the son was Obed, who became the father of Jesse, who became the father of David. In other words, "Ruth the Moabitess," a name that would have generated awful derision, became through faith and love, the great-grandmother of the greatest king of Israel! A lousy Gentile became progenitor of Christ!

Let's see the point here: A person of character, looking for the right qualities in a spouse, and determined to provide the right qualities, can create an unforgettable marriage that brings glory to God. The traits of love, devotion, loyalty, humility, faith, and selflessness made Ruth a "woman of excellence," and a catch beyond all imagination. The simple kindnesses shown by Ruth and by Boaz surely predict the actions that would govern their marriage.

Let us set our minds to be a pillar of strength to our spouses. It may be as brief as Pilate's wife warning him about the righteousness of Jesus, or as long as Jacob laboring for Rachel, but spouses are given to make the world a more bearable place for one another.

My Greatest Encourager

Readings:
- The story of Elkanah and Hannah in 1 Samuel 1
- The whole book of Ruth

Prep questions:
1. What are some of the various ways Elkanah tried to support Hannah?

2. What are some of the temporary storms of life that need a spouse's encouragement?

3. What are some of the longer-lasting storms of life that need a spouse's encouragement?

4. Why is a whole book of the Bible devoted to Ruth?

Chapter Eleven

Job & His Wife, David & Michal, Ahab & Jezebel, Ananias & Sapphira: My Spouse, My Greatest Obstacle

Satan is a cruel and cunning foe. He struck at Job like an expert in the science of torture. He cut Job in the places where it would hurt him the most. But Satan's goal was not pain for pain's sake. Satan wanted to use the pain as a crowbar to separate Job from God.

First, a Sabean raid stole all of Job's livestock and servants. Then, on the very same day, "the fire of God" killed his sheep and hired shepherds. Then, on the very same day, a band of Chaldeans took his camels and herdsman. Then, worst of all, on the very same day, a freak wind caused the oldest son's house to collapse, and all ten of Job's sons and daughters died together.

Any one of these would be enough to cause the strongest man to shatter into a million pieces. Job, however, clung firmly to his faith,

> He said, "Naked I came from my mother's womb, and naked I shall return there. The Lord gave and the Lord has taken away. Blessed be the name of the Lord." Through all this, Job did not sin nor did he blame God (1:21-22).

Satan tried again, with increased intensity. He smote Job with sores from the top of his head to the bottom of his feet. Job took to sitting in a pile of ashes and scraping his skin with a rough shard of pottery.

But in all this misery, there is one individual that Satan did not take away from Job—his wife. Have you ever wondered why Satan did not kill her, like he killed his sons and daughters? Certainly her life was within Satan's power to destroy as well. Wouldn't any one of us trade anything in the world for the life of our spouse? Why didn't Satan cause her death, and blast Job with the painful news?

Perhaps Satan knew that Job's wife was more valuable to Satan's cause alive than dead! He knew that the blow he could inflict upon Job through her words would be sharper than the blow he could inflict upon Job through her death. Satan could use her to tear him down by her presence more than he could use her to tear him down by her absence.

While Job is suffering in the depths of his soul, his wife approached him, in Job 2:9.

> "Do you still hold fast your integrity? Curse God and die!"
> But he said to her, "You speak as one of the foolish women speaks. Shall we indeed accept good from God and not accept adversity?" In all this, Job did not sin with his lips.

Sadly, we never hear her speak again.

Now, before we are too hard on Job's wife, we should understand that she has just lost everything she holds dear, too. She has lost her wealth, the lives of her children, and the health of her husband. She is overwhelmed in suffering. I am not suggesting any of us would be stronger in her situation.

But we do see, through the cunning schemes of Satan, that our spouse is in the unique position of being able to greatly support our faith or greatly undermine it. In just a single sentence, our spouse can save our life or destroy it.

Our spouse can discourage us from taking alcohol and drugs, or can encourage us to experiment with them. Our spouse can hold fast on sexual purity, or can suggest sinful ways to look for fulfillment elsewhere. Our spouse can make it easier for us to go to worship, helping us wake up and get ready, or can make it a lot harder by dragging feet, whining about being groggy, or complaining about the boring nature of the services. Our spouse can be trusted to help us balance the checkbook, or can beg us to run up the credit cards.

This may have been the hardest thing for Job to do, to see his beloved wife's counsel for what it really was—the poison of Satan—and repudiate it. Just as Jesus had to say to His close apostle Peter on one occasion, "Get behind me, Satan!" (Matthew 16:23), Job had to put God before his wife.

I believe it would have been easier for Job to disregard the evil counsel of a hundred friends, than the evil counsel of his beloved wife. At this, most men would throw up their hands and concede defeat. If my wife ever said, "That's it, I cannot stand the preacher anymore; I am never going back to church again," would I have the fortitude to encourage her to reconsider, and if necessary, to continue attending without her?

Without a doubt, a spouse is the single greatest influence on a person's relationship with God.

A Second Example

Another relationship that featured a lot of discouragement was David and Michal in their later years. Now, they had a lot of baggage of the in-law variety. King Saul promised his daughter Michal to any man who defeated Goliath (1 Samuel 17:25–30). David was reluctant to accept this prize (at first, Saul's oldest daughter Merab) until it was pointed out that Saul's daughter Michal "loved David." So, clearly there was a spark at the beginning, when David was growing in popularity. But Saul saw this as an opportunity and demanded 100 Philistine foreskins as a dowry, thinking this quite an impossible task (1 Samuel 18). When David succeeded, he was allowed to marry Michal. But as he continued to distinguish himself, "Saul was David's enemy continually" (v. 29).

Soon, David had to flee into the wilderness. Michal, who remained in Saul's control, was given to another man, named Paltiel, for many years. When David finally conquered the kingdom, he demanded Michal's return (2 Samuel 3:12–16). Poor Paltiel wept and tugged at her hand for miles. It was a mess.

Maybe all this unrest, as well as conflicted loyalties between her husband and her father, caused Michal to lash out at David.

It happened on one of the greatest days in King David's life—he was able to bring the Ark of the Covenant into Jerusalem. He offered sacrifices, blessed all the people, gave gifts to all, and danced and leapt for joy.

> Then it happened that as the ark of the Lord came into the city of David that Michal the daughter of Saul looked out of the window and saw King David leaping and dancing before the Lord; and she despised him in her heart ... But when David returned to bless his household, Michal the daughter of Saul came out to meet David and said, "How the king of Israel has distinguished himself today! He uncovered himself today in the eyes of his servants' maids as one of the foolish ones shamelessly uncovers himself!"
>
> So David said to Michal, "It was before the Lord, who chose me above your father and above all his house, to appoint me ruler over the people of the Lord, over Israel; therefore I will celebrate before the Lord. I will be more lightly esteemed than this and will be humble in my own eyes, but with the maids of whom you have spoken, with them I will be distinguished."
>
> Michal the daughter of Saul had no child to the day of her death (2 Samuel 6:16, 20–23).

Have you ever noticed a married couple constantly bickering and sniping at one another, whether behind each other's backs, or directly to each other's faces? A lack of support from your spouse is one of the greatest vacancies that can exist in your heart. Insults and sarcasm from your spouse hurt worse than any other blow. Satan will use these things to keep a couple from ever reaching the heights of love that God intended. Satan will cause such a marriage to be more memorable for its rancor and animosity than goodwill and intimacy. Satan will use "bitterness and wrath and anger and clamor and slander" (Ephesians 4:31) to cause such a marriage to stand out in the community, but not in a good way. Such marriages often end in divorce, but mostly end in the heart.

As spouses, we have a great responsibility to be a source of scriptural wisdom to our husbands or wives, especially at the biggest moments in their lives.

A Third Example
Perhaps in biblical history there is no bigger "power couple" than Ahab and Jezebel, who used their position as king and queen to bring wickedness and suffering to the people of Israel. There was little strife between them—from all we can tell they were on the same page and happy with one another. Yet, even between these partners in crime, it is clear that Jezebel was the strong one who influenced her husband away from God and toward idolatry.

Ahab was no crown jewel to begin with. The very first thing the Bible says about him is: "Ahab the son of Omri did evil in the sight of the Lord more than all who were before him" (1 Kings 16:30). That's quite an accomplishment. If it were awarded, Ahab would win the Guinness Book of World Records entry for wickedest king of Israel!

The second thing the Bible says about Ahab is:

> It came about, as though it had been a trivial thing for him to walk in the sins of Jeroboam the son of Nebat, that he married Jezebel the daughter of Ethbaal king of the Sidonians, and went to serve Baal and worshiped him. So he erected an altar for Baal in the house of Baal which he built in Samaria. Ahab also made the Asherah. Thus Ahab did more to provoke the Lord God of Israel than all the kings of Israel who were before him (1 Kings 16:31–33).

Ahab already proved himself unconcerned about the ways of God, and ignorant of God's word. Jezebel, however, showed Ahab new ways to commit sin. She introduced Ahab to gods from her native Phoenicia, Baal and his consort, the Asherah. Ahab quickly jumped on the bandwagon to promote the worship of these false deities. The priests of these new gods had official sanction and "ate at Jezebel's table" (1 Kings 18:19). At the same time, Jezebel took it upon herself to hunt down and kill the prophets of God (1 Kings 18:4), apparently by the hundreds, so that Elijah would soon state that he was the last prophet of God standing (18:22). When Ahab coveted Naboth's field, to which he had no right, Jezebel simply "wrote letters in Ahab's name" and had Naboth murdered.

Hand in hand, with Jezebel leading the dance, the pair made it their personal project to provoke God to anger, despite His attempts to remind them of His power and majesty. The Bible sums up the couple's situation,

> Surely there was no one like Ahab who sold himself to do evil in the sight of the Lord, because Jezebel his wife incited him. He acted very abominably in following idols... (1 Kings 21:25, 26).

Finally, Elijah pronounced God's judgment against them both. God caused Ahab to die in battle (1 Kings 22:29–40). A new leader named Jehu eventually eliminated Jezebel, though she tried to charm her way out of her predicament (2 Kings 9:33–37). The dogs licked up the blood of both their corpses, and the worship of Baal was checked, for a while.

Yet, Jezebel's influence lasted longer than her earthly life. Of King Amaziah, their son, it is said, "He did evil in the sight of the Lord and walked in the way of his father and in the way of his mother ... so he served Baal..." (1 Kings 22:52, 53). Successive generations in Judah and Israel struggled with idol worship. Through the corrupt practices of Jezebel's grandchildren and great-grandchildren, the lineage of David was very nearly wiped out (2 Chronicles 21–23).

In fact, Jezebel's influence was so memorable that she became a biblical symbol of false teaching spread through sexuality and idolatry. Jesus said to the church in Thyatira in Revelation 2:20, 21,

> But I have this against you, that you tolerate the woman Jezebel, who calls herself a prophetess, and she teaches and leads My bondservants astray so that they commit acts of immorality and eat things sacrificed to idols. I gave her time to repent, and she does not want to repent of her immorality.

The point is this: in many things, the sum is often greater than the parts. What two can do individually, they often can do much more effectively together. You and your spouse can build a powerful business, but will it be for or against the Lord? You and your spouse can found a powerful organization, or start a family, or develop a hobby, or have a memorable influence on the community; but will these efforts be for or against the Lord? In a worldly sense, Jezebel was a tremendous help to Ahab's success; but in an eternal sense, Jezebel was his greatest obstacle. If a husband and wife help one another dishonor God, they will only be successful in helping one another to Hell.

A Fourth Example
It may even be that a spouse will be put in the uncomfortable position of having to resist his or her spouse in a godly way.

> But a man named Ananias, with his wife Sapphira, sold a piece of property, and kept back some of the price for himself, with his wife's full knowledge, and bringing a portion of it, he laid it at the apostles' feet. But Peter said, "Ananias, why has Satan filled your heart to lie to the Holy Spirit and to keep back some of the price of the land? While it remained unsold, did it not remain your own? And after it was sold, was it not under your control? Why is it that you have conceived this deed in your heart? You have not lied to men but to God." And as he heard these words, Ananias fell down and breathed his last; and great fear came upon all who heard of it. The young men got up and covered him up, and after carrying him out, they buried him. Now there elapsed an interval of about three hours, and his wife came in, not knowing what had happened. And Peter responded to her, "Tell me whether you sold the land for such and such a price?" And she said, "Yes, that was the price." Then Peter said to her, "Why is it that you have agreed together to put the Spirit of the Lord to the test? Behold, the feet of those who have buried your husband are at the door, and they will carry you out as well." And immediately she fell at his feet and breathed her last, and the young men came in and found her dead, and they carried her out and buried her beside her husband" (Acts 5:1–10).

This is often misunderstood as the sin of not putting enough in the collection plate. That's not it at all! Ananias and Sapphira could have placed all, a large percentage, a small percentage, or zero percent of the proceeds of the sale of their land in the collection plate. But, as the previous chapter describes, they had seen Barnabas sell a tract of land and receive adulation, and they seem to have wanted the same kind of attention. Their sin was in lying about the price in order to look good. Imagine if they had sold the land for $10,000, perhaps, but pocketed $2,000 and donated $8,000, claiming that $8,000 was the full price of the land.

While we are not given details behind the scenes, we know Sapphira did not resist her husband's lecherous instincts. Truly, it's a difficult position to be in. What's a Sapphira to do when her husband Ananias is sinning and wants her to join in "with her full knowledge"? Sometimes we become our spouse's best friend when we put our foot down and resist the urge to sin, and encourage faith. It can be tricky both to submit to a husband's leadership and to push him to do better.

Let us dedicate ourselves to being that example of strength at all times, rather than sapping our spouse's spiritual reserves and tearing down his or her defenses. When we compare the actions of the four couples in this chapter, and the two couples in the previous chapter, one thing stands out: Your spouse will be either your greatest support, or your greatest obstacle.

My Greatest Obstacle

Readings:
- The story of Job's losses in Job 1–2
- A couple of statements about Ahab and Jezebel's relationship, in 1 Kings 21:25 and 22:52
- The story of Ananias and Sapphira in Acts 5:1–10

Prep questions:
1. Why didn't Satan kill Job's wife along with Job's children?

2. How was Jezebel able to corrupt so much of life in Israel?

3. How many generations did the influence of Ahab and Jezebel last?

4. What should Sapphira have done in her situation?

Chapter Twelve

Hosea and Gomer:
A Picture of God's Love for the Church

Finish this sentence: "My darling spouse, I love you deeply, but I could never forgive you if you..."
... knocked my golfing trophy off the mantle?
... knocked my golfing trophy off the mantle on purpose?
... told a lie?
... gained 100 lb.?
... sold my boat?
... used the credit cards secretly to rack up $30,000 of debt?
... backed over our two-year-old son with the car and killed him?
... took drugs while pregnant and birthed a handicapped son?
... committed adultery?

Some of these may seem extreme, and yet they are based on real-life examples that I have either known of or heard of. We would probably never voice such a sentiment, but perhaps somewhere deep in the back of our minds we hold onto a list of grievances that we find so terrible, such betrayals of trust, such reversals of character, that we would feel justified in holding onto our rage.

Perhaps the best way to finish the sentence is to first answer a different question: "Why were we married?" Good answers range from "I love her," to "I am attracted to her," to "we have fun together." But they miss out on the biggest and most important reason of all.

Ephesians 5

There are a number of passages in the Bible that, when I run across them again, I get this nagging feeling I am missing something very profound. One such passage is Ephesians 5:31–32, when Paul says,

> For this reason a man shall leave his father and mother and shall be joined to his wife, and the two shall become one flesh. This mystery is great; but I am speaking with reference to Christ and the church.

I don't often think of my marriage as a great mystery, or other married couples as demonstrators of some cosmically significant truth. But that's what Paul asserts. He is inviting us to meditate upon the reasons that God organized mankind into husbands and wives in the first place.

The Greek word *mysterion* does not mean something mysterious or occultish; it means something God reveals to His followers through revelation. *Vine's New Testament Dictionary* says, "In the NT, it denotes not the mysterious, but that which being outside the range of unassisted natural apprehension can be made known only by divine revelation … Its Scriptural significance is truth revealed." In fact, when the word "mystery" is found in the New Testament, it is accompanied by a verb of revelation—words like "made known" or "manifested" or "preached."

In Ephesians 5, God reveals to us the mystery of why He arranged humanity as husbands and wives: to join with one another, to live with one another, to struggle with one another, to disappoint one another, to heal one another, to stand by one another, to sacrifice for one another. Because through this relationship, God can best communicate the depths of His devotion to the church!

Scripture often speaks of God and His people as married. It's helpful to remember that in ancient society there was a year-long legally-binding betrothal period, followed by the marriage feast. Christians are betrothed to Christ, patiently waiting for the feast. In 2 Corinthians 11:2, Paul thinks of himself as a matchmaker, saying, "I betrothed you to one husband, that to Christ I might present you as a pure virgin." When the marriage feast occurs, we will "rejoice and be glad and give the glory to Him, for the marriage of the Lamb has come, and His bride has made herself ready" (Revelation 19:7).

Sin is often described in terms of adultery since one is, spiritually speaking, looking for fulfillment outside his union with Christ. "You adulteresses, do you not know that friendship with the world is hostility toward God?" (James 4:4; *c.f.* 1 Corinthians 6:15; Ezekiel 16:20).

While it is true that we can learn some things about the church's relationship with Christ by considering our marriages, it is much more true that we can learn things about our marriages by considering the church's relationship with Christ.

Hosea

It's a shame that more people are not familiar with the Old Testament Minor Prophets, for the amazing extent of God's love for His church is best discovered in the book of Hosea.

As the book begins, God commands Hosea to "take a wife of harlotry" (1:2). While it is possible that Hosea married a prostitute, it is more likely, and more accepted by the commentators, that she was innocent and pure at the time, and that God was speaking of a future calamity; thus, something like, "go marry a woman who will turn to harlotry," or "a woman who has harlotry on her mind." Whatever the case, her name was Gomer, and Hosea loved her deeply. They soon had a child together.

But Gomer turned (or returned) to a life of harlotry. Perhaps it happened before Gomer's second and third children were born, for these two children were named "No-Compassion" and "Not-My-People." In an age before DNA paternity testing, there would perhaps be nagging suspicion as to whether Hosea had really fathered the children.

While the text does not describe it, we can attempt to imagine the despair, anguish, and anger present in Hosea's heart. He had every reason to have this adulteress stoned to death! Perhaps alone with three children, he struggled with tears and heartache and feelings of betrayal and probably entertained all kinds of feelings of wrath and revenge. Oh, what depths to which Gomer had been reduced, to be a woman with a price! What sin and degradation. What an awful choice! Hosea had just suffered the worst crime that can be committed in a marriage relationship, to an unthinkable degree—to be dumped and publicly shamed not just by a woman with another lover, but with many lovers in an open house of harlotry.

That's why what happens next is so amazing. In one of the shortest and punchiest chapters in the Bible, God said to Hosea,

> "Go again, love a woman who is loved by her husband, yet an adulteress, even as the Lord loves the sons of Israel, though they turn to other gods and love raisin cakes." So I bought her for myself for fifteen shekels of silver and a homer and a half of barley (3:1–2).

God told Hosea, despite all the conflicting emotions in his heart, to settle finally on mercy, and to go find her and rescue her from prostitution. There, he suffered the indignity of having to pay for her release from that situation. He brought her back to his own home and marriage. And after a period of tranquility and rebuilding of trust, of gentle wooing, he received her back as his wife, and he loved her again.

An Illustration of God's Grace

Perhaps of all the charges God gave to the prophets, Hosea's was the most difficult. Isaiah had to walk around mostly naked, and Ezekiel had to lie on the ground for months. But God caused Hosea to experience the heartache of adultery, so that he might communicate to us, in human terms, what God endures when we commit sin. Hosea and Gomer were God's visual aid, God's parable.

God loved Israel, but Israel turned their backs on him and began worshiping other gods with offerings of raisin cakes. God says that if we can imagine what Hosea felt like, we get a good idea of what it feels like to Him when His people, for whom He has done so much, leave Him without cause to return to a lifestyle of filthiness and chaos. The idols of this world offer us far less than what God provides, and yet we pursue them. If we can imagine the feelings of a deserted spouse, we can imagine the feelings of a deserted God. Sometimes we think of sin in clinical terms—like stumbling into poison ivy, and needing to stop at the pharmacy for an ointment to clear it up. In the book of Hosea, we discover that sin is much worse—it breaks the heart of God! Listen to the tossing and turning of God's heart when faced with His people's sin, as recorded in Hosea 11:1–3.

> When Israel was a youth, I loved him,
> And out of Egypt I called My son.
> The more they called them,
> The more they went from them;
> They kept sacrificing to the Baals
> And burning incense to idols.
> Yet it is I who taught Ephraim how to walk,
> I took them in My arms;
> But they did not know that I healed them.

If we can imagine the feelings of a jilted spouse who would decide to search for his missing wife, redeem her from sexual slavery, and be intimate again with his partner who has shared herself with many partners, we can understand the feelings of a God who has bought us from sin at great personal cost to Himself.

Sometimes we think God is above emotions. I'm not so sure. We are, after all, made in the image of God. He reveals a very complex set of feelings toward us, and many religious errors have come from viewing God one-dimensionally; for example, as a God who only loves us with a fawning love, or as a God who is perpetually eager to toss us into hellfire. Passages speak of His anger (2 Samuel 6:6–7), compassion (Mark 8:2), and joy (Luke 15:7).

God speaks of His feelings of hurt and betrayal when His children pursue the world and commit sin. He says in Ezekiel 6:9, "I have been hurt by their adulterous hearts which turned away from Me, and by their eyes which played the harlot after their idols." And of course, God becomes very angry in Hosea 11:5–6.

> ...Because they refused to return to Me
> The sword will whirl against their cities,
> And will demolish their gate bars
> And consume them because of their counsels.
> So My people are bent on turning from Me. ...

And yet, in the same instant, God's heart swings back toward mercy and love, in 11:8–10.

> How can I give you up, O Ephraim?
> How can I surrender you, O Israel? ...
> My heart is turned over within Me,
> All My compassions are kindled.
> I will not execute My fierce anger;
> I will not destroy Ephraim again.
> For I am God and not man, the Holy One in your midst,
> And I will not come in wrath.

God loves His children so much, that even when they commit flagrant and gross sin against Him, and even in the midst of the punishment that they deserve, God's heart turns toward love and mercy.

The Question Again

So, let me ask the question again: What could your spouse do that you could not forgive him for? What could your spouse do that would cause you to say, "I just don't love you anymore"?

When the answer becomes, "Nothing," then we are closer to understanding the love of God. Certainly there are consequences for sin, but a love so deep that it is willing to put aside rage and revenge and pursue forgiveness and reconciliation is God's way. We need to show forgiveness in the many little slights that will punctuate a marriage. And we need to be ready to show forgiveness for the huge sins that will perhaps come along as well.

When we decide to marry another person, we become tremendously vulnerable to that person. That person we trust has the ability to utterly destroy not just our home and finances, but to utterly destroy our hearts. Similarly, when it happens, we are provided the greatest opportunity to plumb the daring depths of forgiveness and redemption. All this allows us to appreciate God's willingness to be hurt and His willingness to forgive.

God took a risk when He created us. When we sin, we don't just violate some impersonal code, we slap the face of God Himself (Hebrews 10:29). He is not just our Creator, but our Father (Matthew 7:9–11). He deeply cares whether or not we love Him and obey Him. He made Himself vulnerable to the chance that we would deny Him and sin. And He knew we would—it's an eternal plan (Ephesians 3:11; 2 Timothy 1:8–9). God knew before He created us that we would reject Him and need salvation—a salvation which could only be provided at great cost to Himself.

God took another risk when He sacrificed His Son for us to redeem us. He took the risk that we would reject Jesus and bring grief to Him (Amos 2:13). He has made Himself vulnerable to our actions. Let us be a source of joy to our God rather than a source of pain.

Hosea teaches us this one great truth: My marriage is not about my satisfaction. It is about doing what is best for my spouse, and thus demonstrating to the world around me the degree of love that Jesus has for His bride, the church. My marriage must be an illustration of Jesus' mercy, love, and grace.

A Picture of God's Love for the Church

Readings:
- The description of Christ's love for the church in Ephesians 5:25–33
- The story of Hosea and Gomer in Hosea 1–3

Prep questions:
1. What is the real "mystery" of marriage?

2. What are some of the feelings God has for His people?

3. What are some of the things God has forgiven you for?

4. Do you think that you *ought* to be able to forgive your spouse for anything? Still, is there something that he or she has done that you have not forgiven him for, or, is there something yet in the future that would challenge you greatly to offer forgiveness?

Chapter Thirteen

∞

Priscilla & Aquila: A Team for Christ

There are some people whose faces I can't imagine without the image of their spouse's face popping up at the same time; whose names I can't say without including their spouse's name, too. Whether sitting on a church pew or on a park bench, they are always together, always devoted, always in love.

Priscilla and Aquila are just such a couple. Every time they are mentioned in the Bible they are mentioned together—every time! It's hard to find a couple more dedicated to the cause of Christ. They are a wonderful example of what a man and woman, devoted to one another and devoted to Christ, can accomplish together.

Priscilla and Aquila allow us to finish our look at impressive couples of the Bible on a very high note. I believe Priscilla and Aquila shows us what a Christian couple can be.

We first meet them in Corinth, in Acts 18:1–4.

> After these things [Paul] left Athens and went to Corinth. And he found a Jew named Aquila, a native of Pontus, having recently come from Italy with his wife Priscilla, because Claudius had commanded all the Jews to leave Rome. He came to them, and because he was of the same trade, he stayed with them and they were working, for by trade they were tent-makers. And he was reasoning in the synagogue every Sabbath and trying to persuade Jews and Greeks.

There are some unknowns. We don't know what brought Aquila to Rome from Pontus (a province far to the north, bordering the Black Sea). Their names don't give us any real insight to their character: Aquila means "eagle" and Priscilla means "little old lady," which was probably more a term of endearment than it sounds today. It is not clear why Claudius drove all Jews out of Rome in 49 or 50AD, though the Roman historian Suetonius suggests it was associated with unrest "at the instigation of Chrestus," likely a reference to Christ and the spread of the gospel. Aquila and Priscilla were Jews, but whether they became Christians before or after they met Paul is difficult to determine.

Much has been made of the unusual fact that Priscilla is mentioned first two-thirds of the time. To students of the New Testament, there's nothing strange or surprising about this. The Bible frequently mentions the contributions of women to the church. In his letters, Paul greets Mary "who has worked hard for you" (Romans 16:6), Tryphaena and Tryphosa who are "workers in the Lord," (Romans 16:12), and Euodia and Syntyche who "shared my struggle in the cause of the gospel" (Philippians 4:2). Paul commends Phoebe as "a servant of the church" and "a helper of many" (Romans 16:1-2), and many scholars believe she was the courier of the Corinthian letter. Clearly, women are not second-class citizens in the kingdom of God.

Paul also praised the teaching that women do (2 Timothy 1:5; Titus 2:3-4). There are moments when it is inappropriate for a woman to teach (1 Timothy 2:11-12) and she will have to be careful not to exceed the position that God has granted her. But the influence of Lois and Eunice is what allowed thousands to be converted by the preaching of Timothy. When we buy apples in the grocery store we may only think of the grocer, but the farmer had the first and most important role in providing that apple. Just so, Lois and Eunice planted the seeds that led to the salvation of many.

The great commission is addressed to women, too. An established Christian woman has a host of skills and knowledge to pass along to young Christian women and those newly converted. She becomes the mother and sister to the new saint (Mark 10:28-31), who is often disentangling from worldly influences.

She can even evangelize. She is in the best position of all to preach the gospel to an unbelieving husband (1 Peter 3:1-2), and to strengthen and voice concern to the struggling husband. Women in the New Testament directly supported the ministry of Christ (Luke 8:1-3). Women also hosted churches in their homes and provided a base of operations for Paul and his fellow workers, as did Lydia in Acts 16:15. They invited others to come and hear Jesus, as did the woman at the well (John 4:28-42).

E. S. Barrett said, "Woman: last at the cross, first at the tomb." It may very well be that women are braver than men when it comes to faith. They were probably converted in greater numbers in all periods of history. In any case, they are equally valued by God (Galatians 3:28), and can look forward to an equal reward.

Busy with Teaching, Together
Although Priscilla and Aquila started working with Paul because they were

in the same tent-making business, they continued working together to spread the gospel. Paul stayed in Corinth for more than 18 months, but after a close call with the authorities, he boarded a ship for home. Pricilla and Aquila came with him (Acts 18:18).

We soon discover why. "They came to Ephesus, and he left them there" (18:19). Paul spent only a few days preaching the gospel in Ephesus. He had to continue home. But he left Aquila and Priscilla to establish the work, hoping to eventually return on his next missionary journey. What great trust Paul had in the faith and diligence of this Christian couple!

When my wife and I were first married, we moved six times in six years. Despite the fact that we had only enough possessions to fit into a single small U-Haul truck, it was never easy. Lugging furniture is bad enough. Uprooting is worse. Moving means leaving friends, jobs, activities, the streets and buildings of a community that you have grown accustomed to, and leaving a home where you can find all the light switches in the dark. Spending the next eleven years in the same house was, in a lot of ways, much more stabilizing and comforting. I don't relish the thought of having to do it again one day.

Priscilla and Aquila were willing to endure the disruption and hardship of moving, which probably meant boarding a boat with few earthly possessions, and starting their business over in a new city, all for the purpose of strengthening the church in Ephesus. I know a lot of people who have moved, but always for personal reasons—new jobs, better weather, better scenery, or to get closer to family. I have met very, very few people who have chosen to move so that they could establish or strengthen a congregation. This would be impossible if a husband and wife were not in complete agreement with putting the work of the Lord ahead of their own desires.

Paul's trust in Priscilla and Aquila soon was proven to have been well-placed.

> Now a Jew named Apollos, an Alexandrian by birth, an eloquent man, came to Ephesus; and he was mighty in the Scriptures. This man had been instructed in the way of the Lord; and being fervent in spirit, he was speaking and teaching accurately the things concerning Jesus, being acquainted only with the baptism of John; and he began to speak out boldly in the synagogue. But when Priscilla and Aquila heard him, they took him aside and explained to him the way of God more accurately. And when he wanted to go across to Achaia, the brethren encouraged him and wrote to the disciples to welcome him; and when he had arrived, he greatly helped those

who had believed through grace, for he powerfully refuted the Jews in public, demonstrating by the Scriptures that Jesus was the Christ (Acts 18:24–28).

It's tricky to figure out exactly what was lacking in Apollos' doctrine. Apparently, he had heard accurate testimony about the life and teachings of Jesus, and, based on his thorough knowledge of the prophecies of the Old Testament Scriptures, became convinced that Jesus was the Christ, the Son of God. He was very zealous in spreading that truth. But, he seemed to be untrained about the purpose of baptism. His doctrine needed some loose ends tied up.

It's truly amazing that Aquila and Priscilla could be the ones to tie them. Imagine: two leatherworkers from the distant frontier feeling brave enough and capable enough to instruct an educated and eloquent man from the most learned and cosmopolitan city on the planet! Apollos was "mighty in the Scriptures," but not so mighty that he couldn't stand to learn something from a humble couple who had been with the Apostle Paul. Thanks to their gentle approach—taking him aside rather than blasting him in the middle of the synagogue—Apollos went on to fully understand the truth and become a powerful force for the Lord in Corinth (1 Corinthians 3:6).

Surely, we all need to keep our minds open to the simple observations and sincere knowledge of other Christians, no matter how educated we think we are. And, we all need to be willing to gently "take aside" a brother who is zealous for the Lord, but needs to have doctrine clarified.

The example of Pricilla and Aquila show us that couples ought to devote themselves to the knowledge of God's word and the teaching of God's word. Couples from humble backgrounds can be more helpful to a congregation's teaching efforts than any well-educated and smoothly-polished speaker. When both spouses are devoted to this work, their effort is even greater. It takes time for my wife to prepare excellent Bible class material, time that I must pick up the slack in other areas of the home. It takes time for me to leave the house in the evening to teach an individual Bible study, time that she must give up when she'd rather be snuggled up on the couch. But sacrificing our own wishes for the greater efforts of the kingdom is what being a faithful Christian is all about.

Devoted to Hospitality, Together

Before long, Paul returned to Ephesus. Priscilla and Aquila were still in Ephesus when Paul wrote the first Corinthian letter from Ephesus, saying,

"Aquila and Prisca greet you heartily in the Lord, with the church that is in their house" (1 Corinthians 16:19).

This reveals yet another element to their great sacrifice for the work of God. They hosted a weekly worship service in their home. Both husband and wife must be thoroughly devoted to hospitality to view this constant intrusion as a blessing. Would any of us enjoy hosting a group meeting month after month? Imagine now hosting not just part of the church, but the whole church, and not just monthly, but weekly! Often when one spouse wants to invite some friends over, there is resistance. It will mean cleaning and organizing, cooking and being "on" for a few hours rather than relaxing in privacy. Hosting required ordering every aspect of their lives—business and leisure and everything in between—according to the priority of the church, its people, and its worship schedule. There would be no staying in bed, no staying home sick, and there would have to be endurance to keep it up with a smile (Romans 12:13). Anyone who has invited brethren over knows why Peter directed us to be hospitable to one another "without complaint" (1 Peter 4:9).

Some months later, when Paul wrote the Roman letter, Priscilla and Aquila had moved back home to Rome. We don't know why, although many historians assume that most of the Jews who once lived in Rome before Claudius's edict trickled back eventually. In any case, true to their pattern, they wasted no time getting involved in spreading the gospel and hosting worship services in their home. In Romans 16:3–5, Paul mentions Prisca and Aquila and says, "greet the church that is in their house."

What a dedicated couple!

Willing to Risk It All, Together
In Romans 16:3–5, Paul also says,

> Greet Prisca and Aquila, my fellow workers in Christ Jesus, who for my life risked their own necks, to whom not only do I give thanks, but also all the churches of the Gentiles; also greet the church that is in their house....

Their service was not without danger. Paul says they "risked their own necks." It's tempting to speculate on the particular scene that Paul may be referring to. While they could have bravely stood with Paul during the troubles and persecutions in Corinth, when he was grabbed by a mob and hauled before the judgment seat of Gallio, the proconsul of Achaia (Acts

18:5–17), there were probably many instances during their time together that are not specifically mentioned in the book of Acts where they had risked their very lives to support Paul's preaching. As it does these days in China and Iran, just having a church meet in one's home risked the violent attention of the authorities. Having their home and property seized might not have been the worst form of persecution.

But it's not just Paul who is thankful for their hard work. "All the churches of the Gentiles" gave thanks to God for His faithful workers, Priscilla and Aquila. Think of how many people owed their salvation to the kindness and boldness of these people!

Individuals can work hard for Christ. We often talk about this man or that woman being a hard worker for Christ. Or we'll talk about "his wife" being a hard worker. But there is something especially beautiful to see a couple completely committed *together* to serving Christ. Just think: what can you and your spouse do together as a team? In 1 Corinthians 7, Paul was concerned that marriage divides a person's interests between pleasing his God and pleasing his spouse—but what if both spouses' main interest is pleasing God? What great things they can accomplish in the Lord's kingdom!

Help one another get to worship. Encourage one another to serve others. Agree to arrange your careers, your family life, even your finances for the Lord. Decide together that instead of retiring to some back porch, you will spend your retirement working for the Lord.

Priscilla and Aquila are two of the people Paul mentions when he writes his affectionate last letter (2 Timothy 4:19), very likely from a cold and damp Roman cell just a few short weeks before he would be executed by a Roman sword. "Greet Prisca and Aquila," he said.

There they are, still very much on Paul's mind, still busy, still beloved, some twenty years after their first meeting.

A Team for Christ

Readings:
- A few glimpses of the work of Priscilla and Aquila in Acts 18:1–28; 1 Corinthians 16:19; Romans 16:3–5

Prep questions:
1. Why does a team accomplish more than two people working individually?

2. What are some things that married Christian couples are especially effective at?

3. What are some sacrifices that would be difficult to make without your spouse's full support and cooperation?

4. Do Priscilla and Aquila deserve some of the "credit" for the conversions that Paul made?

More Bible Study workbooks that you can order from Spiritbuilding.com or your favorite Christian bookstore.

Inside Out (Carl McMurray)
Studying spiritual growth in bite-sized pieces

Night and Day (Andrew Roberts)
Comparing New Testament Christianity and Islam

Church Discipline (Royce DeBerry)
A study on an important responsibility for the Lord's church

Exercising Authority (John Baughn)
How we use and understand authority on a daily basis

Compass Points (Carl McMurray)
22 foundation lessons for home studies, prospects, or new Christians

We're Different Because... (Carl McMurray)
A workbook on authority and recent church history

Communing with the Lord (Matthew Allen)
A study of the Lord's Supper & issues surrounding it

Parenting Through the Ages (Royce & Cindy DeBerry)
Bible principles tested & explained by successful parents

Marriage Through the Ages (Royce & Cindy DeBerry)
A quarter's study of God's design for this part of our life

What Should I Do? (Dennis Tucker)
A study that seeks Bible answers to life's important questions

How To Study the Bible (Jeff Archer)
25 lessons on how to study & understand the Bible

From Fear to Faith (Matthew Allen)
Coming to grips with the doctrine of grace

The Messiah's Misfits (Bryan Nash)
A study of the apostles of Jesus Christ

Living a Spirit Filled Life (Matthew Allen)
A study of Galatians & Ephesians with practical applications

The Lion Is the Lamb (Andrew Roberts)
A study of the King of Kings, His glorious kingdom, & His promised return

When Opportunity Knocks (Matthew Allen)
Lessons on how to meet the J.W./Mormon who knocks on your door

The Last Mile of the Way (Kipp Campbell)
A workbook study of the last week of the Messiah's life

Ancient Choices for Modern Dilemmas (John Baughn)
Biblical view of the modern family, current culture, and American politics

In Search of Christian Confidence (John Baughn)
A study to help one find the confidence God intended for His people

Textual Studies

The Parables, Taking a Deeper Look (Kipp Campbell)
A detailed look at our Lord's teaching stories
That I May Know Him (Aaron Kemple) Vol. 1 & 2
A chronological study of the life of Christ in a harmony of the gospels
1st Corinthians study guide (Chad Sychtysz)
Studies to take the student through this important letter
2nd Corinthians study guide (Chad Sychtysz)
Studies to take the student through this important letter
Hebrews study guide (Chad Sychtysz)
Studies to take the student through this important letter
Romans study guide (Chad Sychtysz)
Studies to take the student through this important letter
Galatians study guide (Chad Sychtysz)
Studies to take the student through this important letter
Ephesian study guide (Chad Sychtysz)
Studies to take the student through this important letter
Philippian, Colossians, Philemon study guide (Chad Sychtysz)
Studies to take the student through these important letters
1 & 2 Timothy and Titus (Matthew Allen)
A commentary workbook on these letters from Paul
Faith in Action: Studies in James (Mike Wilson)
Bible class workbook and commentary on James
From Beneath the Altar (Carl McMurray)
A workbook commentary on the Book of Revelation
1 Samuel (Matthew Allen)
Studying the life and times of this prophet, priest, & judge
Proverbs, Wisdom for Dummies (Carl McMurray)
A workbook study including every verse in Proverbs, divided into topics
An Overview of Isaiah (Chad Sychtysz)
A workbook study of this messianic prophet
An Overview of Jeremiah (Chad Sychtysz)
A workbook study of this prophet
Esteemed of God, Studying the Book of Daniel (Carl McMurray)
Covering the man as well as the time between the testaments
The Minor Prophets, Vol. 1 & 2 (Matthew Allen)
Old lessons that speak directly to us today

Special Interest

The AD 70 Doctrine (Morris Bowers)
The truth about Realized Eschatology

The Holy Spirit of God (Chad Sychtysz)
A diligent, thorough study of this important subject

The Gospel of Forgiveness (Chad Sychtysz)
A presentation of this subject from different biblical angles

Letters to Young Preachers (Warren Berkley)
Letters from older preachers to younger on what they face

Behind the Preacher's Door (Warren Berkley and Mark Roberts)
Issues that preachers will have to deal with

Seeking the Sacred (Chad Sychtysz)
How to know God the way that HE wants us to know Him

Will You Wipe My Tears? (Joyce Jamerson)
Wisdom & resources to teach us how to help others through sorrow

Do Things Well (Warren Berkley and Mark Roberts)
Encouraging and teaching churches to worship with passion

Studies for Women

I Will NOT Be Lukewarm (Dana Burk)
A ladies study on defeating mediocrity

Reveal in Me... (Jeanne Sullivan)
A study to assist ladies in discovering and developing their talents

Will You Wipe My Tears? (Joyce Jamerson)
Wisdom & resources to teach us how to help others through sorrow

Bridges or Barriers (Cindy DeBerry & Angie Kmitta)
Study encouraging harmony with younger/older sisters-in-Christ

Learning to Sing at Midnight (Joanne Beckley)
A study book about spiritual growth benefiting women of all ages

Re-charging Your Prayer Life (Lonnie Cruse)
Workbook for any woman wanting a richer prayer life

Does This Armor Make Me Look Fat? (Lonnie Cruse)
A study of the Christian armor and how it fits women

Heading for Harvest (Joyce Jamerson)
A study of the fruit of the Spirit

Behind Every Good Man (Joyce Jamerson)
Studying the women that stand behind faithful men of today

Forgotten Womanhood (Joanne Beckley)
Studying the traits of godly womanhood

Look Into Your Heart (Joyce Jamerson)
Studying how to calm one's heart, to develop one that is God approved

Studies for Young People

The Purity Pursuit (Andrew Roberts)
Helping teens achieve purity in all aspects of life

Paul's Letter to the Romans (Matthew Allen)
Putting righteousness by faith on a young person's level

Snapshots, Defining Moments in a Girl's Life (Nicole Sardinas)
How to make godly decisions when it really matters

The Path of Peace (Cassondra Givans)
Relevant and important topics of study for teens

Transitions (Ken Weliever)
A relevant life study for twenty-somethings

A Christian's Approach to... (Cougan Collins)
Studies that deal with the issues of life

God's Plan for Dating and Marriage (Dennis Tucker)
Considering God's directions in this vital area

Back to the Beginning (Cougan Collins)
Studying the book of Genesis

Compass Points (Carl McMurray)
22 foundation lessons for youth, home studies, or new Christians

Eye to Eye with Women of the Bible (Joanne Beckley)
Studies for girls of biblical women, good and bad

The Gospel and You (Andrew Roberts)
Helping teens achieve and possess their own saving faith

We're Different Because... (Carl McMurray)
A workbook on authority and recent church history

**Try any of these study workbooks in the
LIVING LETTER SERIES by Frank Jamerson**

The Gospel of Mark / The Gospel of John / Acts
The Letter to the Romans / 1 Corinthians / 2 Corinthians
The Letter to the Galatians / The Letter to the Ephesians
Philippians and Colossians / 1 & 2 Timothy & Titus
1 & 2 Thessalonians / The Letter to the Hebrews
The Letter of James / 1 Peter / 2 Peter and Jude / 1-2-3 John

Other Bible Study Workbooks by Frank Jamerson
The Godhead / Lord, Please Teach Us to Give!
A Study of the New Testament Church
Bible Authority, How Established How Applied

www.ingramcontent.com/pod-product-compliance
Lightning Source LLC
Chambersburg PA
CBHW071305040426
42444CB00009B/1878